Heaven-Haven

I have desired to go
   Where springs not fail,
To fields where flies no sharp and sided hail
   And a few lilies blow.

And I have asked to be
   Where no storms come,
Where the green swell is in the havens dumb,
   And out of the swing of the sea.

                    Gerard Manley Hopkins

Imminent Domain

The Story of the Kingdom of God
and Its Celebration

Ben Witherington III

William B. Eerdmans Publishing Company

Grand Rapids, Michigan / Cambridge, U.K.

Published 2009 by

Wm. B. Eerdmans Publishing Co.

2140 Oak Industrial Drive N.E., Grand Rapids, Michigan 49505 /

P.O. Box 163, Cambridge CB3 9PU U.K.

www.eerdmans.com

Printed in the United States of America

15 14 13 12 11 10 09   7 6 5 4 3 2 1

Library of Congress Cataloging-in-Publication Data

Witherington, Ben, 1951-

Imminent domain: the story of the Kingdom of God and its celebration /

Ben Witherington III.

p.   cm.

ISBN 978-0-8028-6367-6 (pbk.: alk. paper)

1. Kingdom of God.   I. Title.

BT94.W56   2009

231.7′2 — dc22

2008052613

Quotations from the New Revised Standard Version of the Bible (NRSV) are copyrighted ©
1999 by the Division of Christian Education of the National Council of Churches in the
U.S.A. and used by permission.

Contents

Whatever Happened to Kingdomtide?

It was October, and there was something strange about the bulletin. It read at the top "Twentieth Week after Pentecost." Suddenly it dawned on me that we had skipped a whole liturgical season of the church year. Now if we had been following the Jewish liturgical calendar, this would have been quite unthinkable. Everyone knows that after Pentecost and the Feast of Weeks one looks forward to Rosh Hashanah, the Jewish New Year, in the early fall. But because the church has followed the Roman calendar with the New Year celebrated after the winter solstice, we have no such similar event in September or October.

What we are in fact supposed to be celebrating in the early fall is Kingdomtide. This is easily the most unknown or under-observed church season. In part this is because it is the latest of the liturgical celebrations to be added to the church calendar, in the 1930s in fact, and primarily in Methodist and other Protestant Churches. It is normally celebrated beginning on the Sunday closest to August 31, and continues for twelve to thirteen Sundays thereafter, ending with the Feast of Christ the King. But there seems also to be a theological reason for the neglect of this church season. Perhaps it is that we are not at all sure what the Kingdom is, how it differs from the church or from Israel, and thus we are not sure what it is we are supposed to be celebrating. Hopefully this study will provide a partial remedy for this problem as we explore together the realm of God's reign and ask and answer the question: Is it an imminent Domain coming to earth, or should we only look for it in heaven?

KINGDOMTIDE, 2008

The Borders of the Realm

Mention the word "Kingdomtide" in the church today and you are likely to get quizzical looks. The same can often be said if you simply refer to the Kingdom of God. There are probably several reasons for this fact, not the least of which are neglect of the subject in Christian preaching and teaching and the waning of interest in things eschatological in many parts of the church. Yet as a new millennium in church history has now dawned, and even among the general public there seems to be a recognition that we live in difficult and rapidly changing times, there seems to be an increased interest in what shape our future will take. Fortunately, both Kingdomtide as a season and Kingdom teaching have a good deal to say on this subject. It will then be appropriate to take some time now to explore these matters.

Terms of Endowment

Of course the appropriate place to begin our discussion is with definitions, and here already we have two problems. The first is historical. The famous French New Testament scholar Alfred Loisy once said words to the effect that while Jesus preached the coming of the Kingdom, it was the church that showed up. Does this mean that the Kingdom has not yet come or that it came in a form that Jesus did not expect (i.e., as the church)? This historical (and theological) problem can perhaps be resolved if we look more directly at the difficulties of definition at this point.

To most modern people the term "kingdom" always implies a place, whether one is thinking of the United Kingdom or the Magic Kingdom. Yet the Greek term that we often translate "kingdom" *(basileia)* and more importantly the Aramaic term that Jesus likely used *(malkuta)* do not always refer to a place. Sometimes they refer to an activity or a condition instead.

To be more specific, when the Greek or Aramaic word is used in conjunction with "God," sometimes it refers to God's saving activity, sometimes to the resulting condition of that activity in someone's life (namely God's rule in one's life), and sometimes to a place which one enters, inherits, obtains, or is excluded from at the end of human history. In all cases the term refers to something that is part of God's final design or plan for humankind, namely salvation. I would suggest that we use "dominion" instead of "kingdom" since it can refer to an activity (God exercises or has dominion over us and we are in turn ruled by God) or a place (God's Dominion is where the divine rule is manifest). Lest all this sound like an exercise in theological abstractions and mere semantics, we need to remind ourselves that the Dominion of God rather than the church was the featured subject of all of Jesus' parables and much of early Christian preaching. It is thus important for us to get a clear grip on the meaning and importance of this language.

One conclusion will become very apparent as we move along: Jesus and his followers believed that there was an already and a not yet dimension to this Dominion, which in turn meant that they considered themselves witnesses of, heralds of, even bringers of this final or endtime Dominion of God into the world. In their view, the future was now. Jesus put the matter this way: "If it is by the finger of God I cast out demons, then you will know that the Dominion of God has already come upon you" (Luke 11:20/Matt. 12:28). The coming of the Dominion was signaled by the miracles of Jesus and their interpretation by Jesus.

From what we have already said it will be apparent that Kingdom-tide is the celebration of God's final saving activity breaking into our midst and leading us on until "thy Kingdom come, thy will be done, on earth as in heaven." It is appropriate that this celebration takes place in autumn since images of bringing in the harvest or celebrating the harvest with thanksgiving are an integral part of this church season. Joy and gratitude, excitement and a sense of fulfillment are the emotions of and reactions to this season. But the celebration of the Dominion of God will always be an already and not yet affair until the Lord returns. It is rather like the sort of celebration that happens on a wedding day. For the couple involved, once the wedding service has been completed, their marriage is already a present reality and celebration is already in order. Yet there is still in front of them the consummation of the marriage and hopefully a lifetime of happy union together. Similarly the church awaits the consummation of her relationship with her Lord when he returns, but there is already reason to celebrate. God's saving activity has already transpired in our midst such that God has created a people, based on a real and recognized union between the bridegroom and the bride. The already and not yet dimensions of the Dominion of God and of our relationship with God must be kept steadily in view throughout this study. To those who think we have already been blessed with all that a relationship with God can mean we will have to say "Not Yet," but to those who think God's Dominion only has to do with "pie in the sky by and by" we must say "Already!"

Israel, Church, Dominion

Church folk are apt to mistake the Dominion for the church. A moment's reflection will show, however, that the two terms do not refer to exactly the same entity. For one thing, none of us are praying for the church to come, but every time we say the Lord's Prayer we ask God to send his Dominion. For another thing, we don't talk about obtaining or inheriting the church, but we certainly use these terms about God's Dominion. Nevertheless, one can say that God's Dominion can be seen within the church, if by church we mean the people of God. There is a sense in which when God is ruling and saving and transforming his people so that they become the Dominion of God, the church is at least the place where that Dominion can be seen and experienced.

By the same token, Israel and God's Dominion should not be simply identified with one another. If by Dominion we mean God's rule among his people, then wherever God's people can be found, there also is the Dominion. Doubtless Ezekiel was surprised to have his throne-chariot vision while swatting mosquitoes on the River Chebar in Babylon (cf. Ezekiel 1–2), but it was intended as a reminder that God and the divine presence and activity were not confined to Mount Zion in Jerusalem or even to the land of Israel. Furthermore, as the story of Jonah teaches us, God was prepared to accept followers even from among the Ninevites if they repented and honored the one true God. There are also warnings that God's ruling presence can be withdrawn from a group of God's people if they are faithless (cf. Matt. 21:43 and Romans 11). On the other hand, it is clear enough, as we shall see, that Jesus and his earliest followers did expect the final manifestation of God's Dominion on earth to have the land of Israel and the risen patriarchs in that land as its particular focus (see Matt. 19:28; Luke 13:28).

The relationship between the church and Israel is more complicated. All of Jesus' earliest followers were Jews, as of course Jesus was himself. Furthermore, after Easter and Pentecost all the earliest Christians who made up the Jerusalem church were also Jews, so far as we can tell from a close reading of Acts 1–4. There was, then, a time when the church was a subset of Judaism, which took many different forms in the first century A.D.

However, it appears equally clear that most non-Christian Jews came to view Christians as not true Jews, due principally to their belief in and worship of Jesus. On the other hand, the earliest Jewish Christians saw themselves as the very definition of true Jews. By the time we get to what are probably Paul's earliest extant letters, Galatians and 1 and 2 Thessalonians, all written somewhere around A.D. 50, a clear distinction is made between Jews and the followers of Jesus, and even more strikingly Paul applies language previously reserved for Israel to the church. At one point he even calls Jew and Gentile united in Christ, or at least Jewish Christians, "the Israel of God" (Gal. 6:16). Finally, if we read Romans 9–11 carefully it will become apparent that Paul believes that (1) God has not cast off his first chosen people or reneged on his promises to them; (2) nevertheless, those who have rejected Christ or are outside of Christ have been temporarily broken off from the people of God. Not all Jews are true Jews. In the present Paul affirms that a true Jew is one who recognizes Jesus as the Jewish Messiah, as Paul and the other apostles have done. But (3) when the full number of Gentiles become part of the people of God, then Christ will return and "all Israel [i.e., those not already Christians] will be saved" (Rom. 11:26), by which Paul seems to mean a very large number of Jews who hitherto had not believed in Christ.

The upshot of this somewhat complicated discussion is that Israel also cannot simply be equated with the Dominion of God, nor can Israel simply or always be identified with the church, for while sometimes in the New Testament "Israel" may refer to Jewish Christians, most of the time it refers to non-Christian Jews.

It is therefore not surprising that we sometimes get confused about the relationship of God's Dominion, the church, and Israel. What is crucial to bear in mind at this point is that's God's Dominion is a larger concept than either the church or Israel. God's saving activity can happen outside either the Jewish or the Christian community. Indeed, this is what missionary work accomplishes. Needless to say, it can happen outside the nation of Israel, outside the U.S.A., or outside any of the nations that have traditionally had a Judeo-Christian heritage. Furthermore that activity can break into our midst quite apart from our prayers or plans. God and the divine activity cannot be confined or domesticated by God's people. But the New Testament reminds us that God has chosen to activate and implement his eschatological Dominion through one specific person and his activities — Jesus Christ. We will have occasion to say much more on this subject later.

Thus, at Kingdomtide, we are celebrating the great saving acts of God throughout salvation history, but especially those which began with the coming of Jesus. This divine activity, which resulted in a gathered people of God, is cause for celebration, not least because it reminds us that God and the divine plan are larger than we could ever imagine. It cannot be confined to a particular time of year, a particular denomination, a particular church, a particular country, or a particular age.

Since the coming of Christ, the world has indeed been living in the eschatological age, the age in which God's final saving blessings are made available already, at least in part. The end times are not merely near but are already here ever since the Messiah came to earth. Yet, there is never a time when the Dominion is so fully present that we do not need to continue to pray "Thy Kingdom come, thy will be done, on earth as it is in heaven." God's Dominion or reign is only perfectly manifested at present in heaven, which is also God's realm. While God's reign is manifested from place to place and time to time on earth now, it cannot be said that his realm can yet be fully found on earth. It is this to which Christians look forward when they reflect on the meaning of Kingdomtide and pray "Thy Kingdom come."

Our task in this brief study is to unpack some of the issues discussed above more fully and develop their implications for us in the church today. The study will be divided into two parts with three chapters each. Part One, entitled "The Powerful Presence," will focus on the reality of God's Dominion as it manifests itself in the present. Chapter

One, called "The Design of the Dominion," will deal with how the Dominion is present in our world today and what this might mean for the life of the Christian and of the church. Chapter Two, entitled "The Place of the Presence," will focus more directly on where God's Dominion may now be found. It will deal with the issue of how Jesus was in a sense the locus of the Dominion while on earth and how his body is that location now. Chapter Three, "Taking the Presence Personally," addresses the questions of where and in what manner the Dominion is present in the individual Christian's life.

Part Two, entitled "The Glorious Future," deals not surprisingly with the aspect of God's Dominion that lies ahead of us and is yet unrealized. Chapter Four, "Thy Kingdom Come," will focus on how God's full reign will be fulfilled on earth and how this is related to the issue of dying and going to heaven. Chapter Five, entitled "Thy Will Be Done," deals with the issue of the extent of the Dominion, the nature of the new Jerusalem, and the future of Israel. The implications of this teaching for interfaith dialogue will be explored. Chapter Six, called "On Earth as It Is in Heaven," will deal with the future of the world itself and ask what God's plan is for nature and how this might affect our ecological vision. How does all of this affect our vision of God's presence in the world and our response of gratitude and good stewardship to that presence?

It is my hope that this brief study will spark an ongoing exploration of the importance of the Dominion of God for the church and for the individual Christian and at the same time will help us to see the validity and indeed importance of celebrating this reality in Kingdomtide. If this goal is achieved, I will be content. For now, for those of us who live in the in-between times, in the time between the first and second coming of Christ, the watchword about God's Dominion on earth must be Already! but also Not Yet!

Questions for Reflection and Discussion

The Introduction deals with matters of definition, and seeks to distinguish God's Dominion from the church and from Israel.

☙ Why has the term "Dominion" been chosen instead of "Kingdom"?

☙ If you had to choose, would you expect it to be more likely to find the Dominion of God within the confines of the land of Israel or in the context of the church or perhaps somewhere else?

☙ Why do you suppose Kingdomtide is the most neglected season of the church year?

Part One

THE POWERFUL PRESENCE

CHAPTER ONE

The Design of the Domain

Here we will deal with the manner in which the Dominion of God has come into human lives ever since Jesus walked among us. The heart of this matter is a matter of the heart, as we shall soon see. God's design was to begin the renewal of the world by re-creating human beings in the divine image, by saving and transforming human lives one after another. This was done not in the abstract but with a concrete model. Christ was the model of the Dominion of God on earth, and it is as we are conformed to his image through God's saving activity in us that we become Christ-bearers and Dominion-bearers to others.

At one point in Luke's presentation of Jesus' teaching, the Pharisees are reported to have asked Jesus when the Dominion of God was coming. The response given is "The Dominion of God is not coming with things to be observed; nor will they say, 'Look, here it is!' or 'There it is!' For in fact the Dominion of God is in your midst" (Luke 17:20-21). The Pharisees' question is quite understandable. They expected that there would be clear visible signs or evidence of the Dominion's coming, signs like the resurrection of the righteous, the appearance of a messianic figure that would cast Israel's enemies out of the land, the renewal of the land of Israel itself. Jesus is suggesting that the Dominion is already present during his ministry, but the visible signs of it are not as expected or as advertised.[1] Indeed, the only visible signs of it during Jesus' ministry were changed human lives, the impact Jesus' words and miraculous deeds had on those who encountered him. This is very much the situation of the Dominion today. Lives are still being changed by the proclamation and application of the Good News, but the fallen world as we know it continues without any other visible signs of transformation.

What Jesus told these Pharisees raises important issues for us about the reign of God. If Christians around the world are praying each day "Thy Kingdom come, thy will be done," does this not imply that in fact the Dominion has largely *not* come on earth? Does it not imply that God's plan for humankind has failed to be fully implemented in the first 2000 years of church history? Is this not precisely why so many church people are wary of end-time predictions and promises of zealous fundamentalist evangelists?

It could be said that the one thing such prophets of imminent doom and the approaching end of the world have in common down through the ages is that they all have a perfect track record. They have all been wrong! Their mistake is that they have reduced proper Christian expectations to calculations and prognostications, which is a violation of the very general nature of such prophecies and promises. Not only did Jesus tell us that not even he knew when his return would occur and with him the Dominion of God would fully come on earth (Mark 13:32), the truth is that God has chosen only to reveal enough about the future to give us strong hope and assurances (see Heb. 11:1) but not so much that we do not have to live by faith. Does this then mean that Alfred Loisy was right that for the present the Kingdom has not come but only the church has shown up?

---

1. This text should not be translated "The Kingdom of God is within you" as Jesus is certainly not saying that God's reign is evident within the lives of the adversarial Pharisees with whom he is dialoguing.

These are difficult questions, and it is not hard to understand why some Christians as well as most non-believers have tuned out apocalyptic prophets and preachers and ignored or repudiated or tried to transform the eschatological language of the New Testament into some more palatable form of discourse. Yet those who do so have clearly missed the point of Jesus' words in Luke 17:20. Jesus warned that God's Dominion, as it began to come on earth, would not be evidenced by dramatic visible signs in the sky or the end of the world. To the contrary and no doubt to the shock of the Pharisees, Jesus was saying that the Dominion was already in their midst and that they were missing it! What was it then that they were missing? They were overlooking the very same thing that millions of people overlook today when they assume that God's Dominion will only come in the form of dramatic signs in the heavens and wonders on the earth.[2]

God's Dominion on earth is a cipher for God's final divine saving activity that happened first through the ministry of Jesus and then continuously through the ministry of his followers over the course of the last two millennia. The essence of this is that God sets up the divine reign in the lives of those who receive him. It is what Christians are referring to today when they talk about Christ ruling in their hearts or being Lord of their lives. The Dominion has come to the most personal and private of locations — into the inner lives of individual human beings and into the midst of the community of God's people. Yet that is not all, for as we shall see, changed lives lead to redemptive actions, which in turn change other lives and even to a real degree can on occasion change the very fabric and structure of a society.

For some, the notion of the coming of the Dominion of God within the human heart will seem far too small and cramped a space for God

---

2. This sort of expectation today is not surprising in view of the enormous appeal today of science fiction, Star Wars movies, and the like. The future beckons and we long to look into it.

to work, if God's saving activity is going to make a difference in the world. It will appear to some that this is an over-spiritualizing of the concept of God's Dominion. Is this being too heavenly-minded to be any earthly good?

While such a reaction is understandable, it fails to come to grips with the fact that most of the major problems human beings face in life originate in the human heart. Whether we think of war, murder, adultery, drug addiction, theft, idolatry, or racist or sexist acts, all these horrors ultimately originate in the human heart. Jesus understood this and at one point condemned the lusts of the heart (Matt. 5:27-28). God's saving Dominion comes to deal with the primary source of human social maladies, not simply to deal with the social effects or communal expressions of such maladies, though responding to the latter is also important.

Elsewhere, Jesus is also reported to have remarked, when discussing the issue of clean and unclean food, "whatever goes into a person from outside cannot defile, since it enters not the heart but the stomach. . . . It is what comes out of a person that defiles. For it is from within, from the human heart, that evil intentions come: fornication, theft, murder, adultery, avarice, wickedness, deceit, licentiousness, envy, slander, pride, folly" (Mark 7:18-22). In sum, in Jesus' view the heart was the heart of the matter, and humankind desperately needed a heart transplant or transformation, not merely a bypass operation. Dealing simply with behaviors is dealing with the symptoms and manifestations of the problem, not its source.

In both the Old and the New Testaments, the human heart is seen as the control center of human personality. It is where one finds thoughts, emotions, and will. This is why, for instance, we hear about the "thoughts of the heart" in the Bible. God knows that if the control center of human personality can be gotten hold of and pointed in the right direction, then the rest of the person and personality will follow. It is very much like leading a horse to water. If the halter is on the horse and one can get hold of it and turn the horse's head, the rest of the horse will follow. So too with human beings. Once God gets hold of a person's heart, the renovation of the whole person has been set in motion. When the heart is led in a particular direction, the rest will follow.

Here I would like to offer two illustrations of my point about the importance of the reign of God's saving activity in the human heart. First, a laudable campaign against drugs in the public schools had as its slogan "Just Say No." The assumption was that better informed young people and sufficient exhortation should give them the gumption to reject turning to drugs. The problem with this assumption is that information without inner transformation will not and cannot finally solve the problem. The human heart must be changed if people are really to be different. A new attitude and will, not just new ideas, are required. If we really want to end the drug problem in America we would do well not merely to preach but also to pray that God's transforming, saving activity might break into the lives of those who are addicted to one or another drug.

Recently, I had occasion to see a powerful play by a man named Stephen Dietz entitled "God's Country." It deals with the still pervasive problem of racism in our society. Racism is one of our society's perpetual besetting sins, perhaps because we have always been an immigrant nation, with lots of new faces, and quite naturally self-centered human beings are suspicious of those who do not look, dress, speak, or act like themselves. All human beings tend to assume that they are normal and that others not like them are therefore strange, suspicious, or even wicked. Dietz drives home the point that racism originates in the human heart, and more to the point that racism is based on and driven by the irrational fears and illogical assumptions that often reside in the heart.

It is precisely because human beings are fallen creatures and their thoughts and feelings are often dark and dangerous that God's Dominion must first invade and take over the human heart if human society is to be improved. Jesus understood this and proclaimed the Dominion in such a way that people could realize that God demands and delivers a personal change in people's lives when he comes to dwell in fullness within them and in their midst. This leads not just to the power of positive thinking but to a transformed will and healed emotions.

Of course the essential presupposition of all this proclamation of the need of God's saving presence in a human life is that human beings are not all right in their present condition. The presupposition is that human beings are fallen and cannot get up by their own efforts. They are lost in a world of self-centered and self-seeking ventures and realities and require a radical rescue operation to be set right so that they may truly learn to love others and become other-directed individuals. What the Dominion of God entering the heart does is to take a person out of a circus-like hall of mirrors environment where one is perpetually looking at and admiring various configurations of oneself and to place that person out in the fresh air of God's world where he or she may see the world as it is and understand his or her own place in it.

Paul, like Jesus, spoke of the Dominion of God in the present tense as a reality in the here and now. For example, in Romans 14:17 Paul says, "The Dominion of God is not food and drink but righteousness and peace and joy in the Holy Spirit." In other words, the Spirit forms these qualities in the life of the believer, and they become evidence that God's saving activity has been at work in this person's life, evidence that the Holy Spirit has taken up residence in this person. Of course, the evidence that God has worked in the believer will be manifested in the believer's relationships in the Christian community and with the world. Righteousness, "shalom" (peace), and joy all manifest themselves in deeds and relationships. The starting point, however, is the transformed inner life of the individual.

Our discussion thus far raises some important questions about God's work and will for humankind. It raises questions about what might be God's plan for a person's life. In the broad sense these questions are easy to answer. God desires that all persons be saved, that all be conformed to the image of Jesus' character, that all in short become their best selves. Paul states the matter succinctly: "This is the will of God: your sanctification" (1 Thess. 4:3). God is a holy and loving God and desires to create a holy and loving people. This is what adequately reflecting God's image on earth means. When God's character is reflected in our character in our daily lives, then the Dominion of God is evident on earth. Then God's will is being done on earth as it is already being done in heaven.

But human beings cannot survive outside human society, and in fact human beings cannot survive outside a certain kind of ecosystem. We need oxygen, water, sunlight, food, clothing, and a host of other things to survive. It is not surprising then that God's plan for our ultimate future includes not just saved individuals but also a renewed earth, a matter we will have occasion to discuss later in this study.

If, however, the Dominion of God in the present is chiefly about our becoming holy persons, many will perhaps be dismayed by how far short of God's holiness they fall. This reaction is both understandable and proper. We do sin and fall short of God's best for our lives. But we need to understand that salvation, or God's saving activity in our lives, is a matter of grace, not something we earn. This is why Jesus reassures his followers by saying "Do not be afraid, little flock, for it is your Father's good pleasure to give you the Dominion" (Luke 12:32). The Dominion in our lives comes as a gift, not as something we have earned, and its effects, including holiness, are likewise also a gift. Yet, once it has been given, it requires of us our all to manifest it and live it out. "No one who puts a hand to the plow and looks back is fit for the Dominion of God" (Luke 9:62).

God does not implement the divine plan in the abstract or on a purely spiritual plane. God's Dominion comes to pass through persons and in persons. In particular God's plan is implemented through Jesus Christ. There is a sense in which Jesus was not just the revelation of

God's will while he was on earth, but the implementation of that will. Jesus embodied the will of God and delivered God's divine saving presence to others. In an analogous way, we embody the Dominion of God for others by reflecting the character of Christ. Through our words and hands and actions various people can be saved, can come to have a relationship with Christ as their Lord.

Through Jesus, and then through those who are in Christ, the Dominion came and comes. For example, consider the saying we find in Matthew 12:28: "If it is by the Spirit of God that I cast out demons, then the Dominion of God has come to you." What this means is that Jesus is the agent through whom God's saving activity happens, and one of the effects of this activity is healing, which in this case takes the form of deliverance from the powers of darkness. The Dominion of God is so powerful that not even other competing supernatural forces can stop it from coming and delivering human beings from the things that bewitch, bother, and bewilder them. God desires for us to be both well and whole, and through his Son he takes a holistic approach to salvation — it involves both the human spirit and the human body, both the mind and the flesh, both the emotions and the actions, both the will and the doing. The focus, however, of this divine activity is on the human heart, which is, as we have said, the control center of human personality.

We live in a world that, after two world wars in the last century and various lesser conflicts ever since, has a rather jaded view of the future. In fact, many people including many of our young people could be called people without hope. The analogue of this loss of hope for the future is a sort of *carpe diem* or "seize the moment" approach to life. You hear this attitude in slogans like "He who hesitates is lost" or "The early bird gets the worm" or even "You only go around once in life so grab all the gusto you can get." This sort of tunnel vision or over-fixation with the present is part of the malaise we call postmodernism. Some have thought that the only solution for such a narrow field of focus is to speak in dramatic or shocking or winsome ways about the future to jolt people out of their narcissism.

It is interesting that Jesus would not have entirely agreed with this logic. To be sure, some of his message to his own people, many of whom had abandoned hope because of the crushing tyranny of Roman rule, did have a future dimension to it. The Dominion of God was not fully present, and so Jesus taught his disciples to pray "Thy Kingdom come . . . on earth," which meant that it was most certainly not fully here. But at the same time, as we have already seen, both Jesus and Paul were also saying "the future is now."

Already God's divine saving activity was breaking into their midst. Already human lives were being changed and a new community of believers was being formed. Already the sick were being healed, already the blind were gaining sight, already the lost were being found. Jesus did not come just to announce the coming of God's saving reign upon the earth, he came to inaugurate it. Yet this Dominion was not like the kingdoms of this world.

The famous encounter between Jesus and Pilate reminds us that while God's Dominion is manifested in this world it is clearly not this-worldly in character (John 18:36). Jesus says that if it had been just another human kingdom his own disciples would have fought to bring it into reality. Indeed, to the untrained and unspiritual eye it might seem that it was not coming at all, for there was no capital of this Dominion, no army to protect this Dominion, no political negotiations in this Dominion. This Dominion is about the redemption of persons which is often an invisible, or not immediately apparent affair.

When Columbus approached King Ferdinand and Queen Isabella about finding a new passage to the Orient, the motto on the Spanish flag was "Ne Plus Ultra," which means "there is nothing beyond" (in this case nothing beyond the realm of the Spanish Empire). Yet in 1492, quite apart from what Columbus was looking for, the New World was found. Thereafter it became apparent that the motto of the Empire needed to be changed. It needed to read "Plus Ultra" — there is more beyond. This last is in a sense the message of the Gospels and especially of texts like the one with which we began this chapter — Luke 17:20. Jesus was saying, there is already more here in your midst than meets the eye, there is more beyond what is empirically in evidence. The only visible evidence of this inbreaking Dominion was changed human lives.

But what God is doing now in our lives is but a foretaste of things to come, a preview of coming attractions. To the thief on the cross who asked to be remembered when Jesus came into his Dominion, Jesus replied, "I say to you, today you will be with me in Paradise" (Luke 23:43). It is interesting that in Luke's Gospel these are Jesus' last words to another human being before his death. The Dominion was on Jesus' mind right to the end, and he believed it had a future, however glorious some of the present manifestations of the Dominion might have been. Jesus' motto was "Plus Ultra," there is more beyond.

For a jaundiced world that thinks there is nothing new under the sun and nothing to look forward to in life, the gospel of God's Dominion offers a rebuttal. It suggests that there is grace here and glory hereafter if one will set one's eyes on God's Dominion rather than on human realms and reigns. Adoniram Judson, the famous missionary to Burma, was right when he told a pagan tribal chieftain, even as the latter was about to kill Judson, that the future was as bright as God's promises. Jesus said as much when he reassured us all that it is God's will to give us the Dominion of God, in part now, in full later.

Christians have often been accused of peddling a message of pie in the sky by and by, but what we have learned in this chapter is that the Dominion of God, the divine saving activity of God, the reign of God in human lives has already been happening in our midst through the work of Jesus and the Holy Spirit. Therefore, God has a track record. We look forward to the future based on what we know God has accomplished for us in the past and is accomplishing in the present. In Christ we have been saved, we are being saved, and we shall be saved. In our next chapter we must raise and answer the question more specifically — Where is the Place of the Dominion's Presence? It is a question to which our fallen world desperately needs to know the answer.

Questions for Reflection and Discussion

Chapter One introduces the reader to the concept of God's Dominion as a reality in the present, as something surprising that does not come with observable signs other than the changed lives of those who receive it.

- ☞ How is a person's life different when God begins to reign or be Lord in his or her life?
- ☞ What is God's will for a human life?
- ☞ What is Jesus' role in implementing the coming of God's Dominion?
- ☞ Why is the human heart such a target in God's plan to change the world?
- ☞ What does the prayer "Thy Kingdom come" tell us about the present dimensions of God's divine saving activity?

CHAPTER TWO

The Place of the Presence

W e have thus far considered the definition and nature of God's
Dominion on earth and how it operates in our midst. Building
on these insights we must now ask where that Dominion can be found
on earth. What is the relationship of the church to the manifestation of
God's Dominion on earth? In what ways can the church better manifest
that Dominion? What is the difference between a church that has a
Kingdom mentality and a church that manifests the Dominion? These
are the issues we will address in this chapter.

If Jesus had been questioned about the location of God's Dominion
during his ministry, he might well have responded, "It's hiding in plain
sight." This is in fact the gist of several of his parables. For example, in the
parable of the mustard seed he compares the Dominion to the sowing of a
seed that later grows and produces a large mustard bush (Luke 13:19), or
again he draws an analogy with the hiding of yeast in a mass of dough
(Luke 13:20) or the sowing of wheat seed in a field (Mark 4:1-9). In all these
parables, the Dominion is seen as present and yet hidden to the naked eye.

During his ministry Jesus meant that God's divine saving activity
or rule, which is the Dominion of God, could be partially seen in the
lives of those whom Jesus healed, helped, or saved or those in whom he
planted the seed of the Word, which only later would manifest God's
reign in their lives. But there is another sense in which Jesus may have

seen the Dominion of God as present during his own time. When he told the Pharisees that God's Dominion was not coming with signs that could be observed but that nonetheless the Dominion of God was in their midst (Luke 17:20), hiding in plain sight, he may well have been referring to himself. He was the place where God's rule, God's saving activity, God's Dominion could be seen to be present in a fallen world. He was the locus of saving grace and divine power overruling the powers of darkness. Those who came into contact with him came into contact with God's Dominion, whether they realized it or not.

Paul likewise, when he speaks about where one can find the Dominion of God in the world in the present, speaks of qualities manifest in Christians' lives that make it clear that Christ and Christ's likeness is within them through the work of the indwelling Holy Spirit. "The Dominion of God is not food and drink but righteousness and peace and joy in the Holy Spirit. The one who thus serves Christ is acceptable to God and has human approval" (Rom. 14:17-18). The Dominion involves not just inner qualities but also outward actions that bring about righteousness, peace, and joy in this world.

What is implicit in the teaching of both Jesus and Paul on this subject is that the Dominion of God in the present cannot be limited to a specific locale such as the Holy Land or any other place. It will be found wherever God's transforming Spirit is at work throughout the world. Paul and Jesus saw that work as happening through the proclaiming of the Good News and through acts of help and healing performed by the followers of Jesus and in his name.

Since we still live in the time between the inauguration of God's Dominion on earth and the full bringing of that Dominion to earth when Christ returns, there is a sense in which we live in very much the same situation as Jesus' and Paul's first disciples. We also need to hear the exhortation of Jesus to be looking for God's Dominion not through signs in the heavens and the like, but wherever the work and grace of the gospel is administered.

Of course this will mean that God's Dominion can be found within the context of God's people, the church. There preeminently one would expect to find the Good News proclaimed and lives being saved, helped, and healed. But it is a mistake simply to identify God's Dominion with the church. God's saving activity happens among the people of God, but of course it also happens when missionaries go to places where the gospel has not been shared before and there are no assemblies of believers. If salvation can be taken to the lost quite apart from the context of the gathered body of Christ, then of course the church and the Dominion of God cannot be synonymous, for "the Spirit blows where it wills." Just as Jesus was not prepared to identify Israel in his day with God's Dominion but rather sought to bring that Dominion into the midst of Israel so that Israel could be redeemed, so likewise, while God's Dominion does break into the context of the gathering of Christians, it does so also where Christians scatter for service and ministry.

How then does the church show that God rules its life, that God has transformed a particular group of people? The answer to this question is complex. First, corporate worship can be pointed to as a clear sign that a particular group of people recognize the sovereignty of God, that God is the ruler of the universe and we are not. In worship, we recognize God as God and ourselves as God's creatures and thus as less than God. True worship makes clear the Creator-creature distinction and implies that we humans should not be seen as objects of worship. Only God — Father, Son, and Holy Spirit — deserves to be worshiped and so recognized as sovereign in the universe. True worship is the opposite of idolatry, which by definition is the worshiping of someone or something as God that is in fact less than and other than God.

Second, the church gives evidence that God is in its midst when Christian individuals and groups of Christians have the qualities that are the result of God's presence in a human life — love, joy, peace, patience, kindness, goodness, self-control, righteousness, and holiness, and many more such qualities could be listed. Basically, when one sees the character of God in Christ in a person's life, one sees the evidence of God's Dominion in that person. But again these are not abstract qualities but traits that reveal themselves in works of piety and charity.

When we think of works of piety, we think for instance of prayer, a clear sign that a person is seeking the help of a higher power and so seeking to properly align himself or herself according to the will and under the rule of God. We may also think of confession as a proper work of piety that manifests the Dominion of God. For example, Paul says that a saved person, one transformed by Christ's divine saving activity, is one who has confessed that Jesus is Lord and believed that God raised him from the dead (Rom. 10:9). Such a person is manifesting the rule or Dominion of God in his or her life.

But it is not just by acts of devotion that a person manifests the Dominion in his or her life. In 1 John 3:24 we hear that all who obey God's commandments (specifically believing in Jesus and loving each other) abide in God and God abides in them. Obedience to God's Word is a sign of the presence of God's reign in a person's life. And the opposite of obedience to God's commandments is taken as a clear sign that one has not experienced God's rule or saving activity in his or her life. "Do you not know that wrongdoers will not inherit the Dominion of God? Do not be deceived! Fornicators, idolaters, adulterers, male prostitutes, sodomites, thieves, the greedy, drunkards, revilers, robbers — none of these will inherit the Dominion of God" (1 Cor. 6:9-10). Here Paul is speaking about the future dimension of God's Dominion, when it fully comes on earth, but the point is that such patterns of behavior now lead to exclusion then and there. Of course, since Paul is warning his Christian audience at this point, he is reckoning with the possibility that Christians can and do sin, even sin against the saving presence within their lives. His concern is that such behavior, if persisted in, can lead to exclusion from God's presence and Dominion in the end.

In deeds of charity, deeds of righteousness, or deeds of love, we may also see the presence of God's Dominion on earth. Obviously the primary deed of love that one can do for a fallen world is to share the gospel with that world. The early church understood that God's Dominion would be spread on earth by evangelism and missionary work. But there are, of course, other valid ministries of love, such as helping the poor or the sick, such as Mother Teresa spent her life doing, or building Habitat for Humanity houses, or collecting funds for famine relief, or supporting a child through Christian Children's Fund.

It is important to stress, however, that God's Dominion is also evidenced through deeds of righteousness, whether opposing racism or sexism, working for fairness and equality in the workplace, seeking to reform the justice system to make it more equitable, or working for tax reform that ensures that the helpless and handicapped in our society are taken care of. Bishop Peter Storey, the Methodist bishop in South Africa who along with Desmond Tutu and others opposed apartheid by nonviolent means until the system was abolished, tells many moving stories of the cost of discipleship in that situation, the cost of manifesting God's Dominion on earth. His sons faced imprisonment for refusing to serve in the army, which enforced apartheid, and he on various occasions faced down the guns in order to protect others. On one particular occasion he tells of being taken with Desmond Tutu out into the woods beyond Johannesburg in order to be shot. But as the young men were about to fire the bishop yelled out: "Are you Christians?" When they responded that they were, then he told them they could not do this heinous act, and, shaken by that rebuke, they stood down and let the two men live.

In a fallen world, the Dominion of God will always be opposed by the powers of darkness. Real transformation often comes in society very slowly and painfully. What is important about the stories that Bishop Storey and others tell is that they make clear that it is not enough for God to reign in the human heart. That Dominion must manifest itself in everyday human behavior, in human relationships, in society. God demands of us a bold witness for Christ and a prophetic witness against evil and injustice.

How then can the church better be a place where God's Dominion is manifest? First it must seek to be a fellowship of the transformed. It must manifest the character of God within its own fellowship and in its dealings with the world. "Those who say, 'I love God,' and hate their brothers or sisters, are liars; for those who do not love a brother or sister whom they have seen, cannot love God whom they have not seen" (1 John 4:20). In short, the church must be a place where Kingdom qualities are in evidence. There can be no place for rivalry or racism, segregation or sexism, greed or graft in the church. Righteousness must be our garment, justice our goal, love the means to all such ends.

The church must be prepared to ask itself hard questions if it wishes to be a city set on a hill setting an example of Godlike qualities and divine reign for the world. For example, it must ask why the 11 o'clock worship hour remains the most segregated hour of the week in America. Why do churches so often see benevolence ministries and collections for the poor as burdens rather than opportunities to bless? Why do most churches in North America spend up to 90 percent of their budgets on their own buildings, their own pastors, on programs that chiefly benefit themselves, rather than on deeds of mercy or on sharing the gospel outside their walls? The early church was a missionary movement that also nurtured those already among the saints. The modern church is a nurture institution that may have a mission committee or budget. The question is, which better manifests God's will and Dominion in our midst?

When Jesus told stories about who would sit down at the messianic banquet when the Dominion of God fully came on earth, he reminded his followers that there would be some surprising people present. "I tell you that many will come from the east and the west and will eat with Abraham and Isaac and Jacob in the Dominion of Heaven while the heirs of the Dominion will be thrown into outer darkness" (Matt. 8:11; cf. Luke 13:28-29). The question such strong warnings raise for us is whether the church is a winsome place. Is it a place that the least, the last, and the lost find inviting and helpful? Is it a place where the least, the last, and the lost become the first, the most, and the found? Is the church, any church, a hospital for sick sinners or a museum for saints? Doing a better job of ministering to its community is one way a church can better manifest God's Dominion.

Yet another way this can happen in the present is by having powerful life-transforming worship and potent life-directing teaching and fellowship so that people will be eager to come back week after week and draw close to God. "I was glad when they said to me, 'Let us go into the house of the Lord.'" As the psalmists say repeatedly and in various ways, God dwells in the midst of the people's praises. Vital worship and fellowship is itself a clear manifestation of God's saving presence. Though the early church had many faults, it does not appear to have suffered from being boring. The description of worship in 1 Corinthians 11–14 suggests it involved singing, prophesying, preaching, speaking in tongues, praying, sharing in the Lord's Supper, eating a fellowship meal, listening to teaching and evaluating it, sharing words of encouragement, sharing news from the mission field, opening one's house for fellowship meetings, and a host of other things. There is only one report in the New Testament of someone going to sleep during worship, and this was because the preacher went on late into the night, not because the service was dull. Early church worship was a happening that took several hours to complete, and few were eager to leave when it was over.

A further way that a church can manifest God's Dominion is by having a solid ongoing commitment to witnessing in its own community and supporting missionary work throughout the world. Jesus, when asked to speak about the future, said that before God's will could be fully done on earth, before Christ could return, "the gospel must first be proclaimed to all nations" (Mark 13:10). Matthew's Gospel concludes with the Great Commission to make disciples of all nations (Matt. 28:19-20). It is a question as to how seriously we take these remarks. There are still hundreds of language groups who do not have the Word of God available in their tongue, and yet Wycliffe Bible Translators and other such valid ministries are always short of support for translating and sharing the Scriptures. What would the church look like if it really took seriously the Great Commission? It would look a lot more like the Dominion of God coming on earth.

Jesus once remarked that the primary family for his followers must be the family of faith, not the physical family, indeed, that whoever did God's will, who manifested God's Dominion, was his brother, sister, and mother (Mark 3:31-35). A church where the Dominion is in evidence is a church that not merely nurtures nuclear families, but indeed is a family to all its members. We live in a world full of broken relationships and many single people. They are looking for love and support and help and in some cases healing. If the church is being a family, then all people, not just married people, will find it a place where God's saving and redeeming activity is in evidence. What sort of message is the church sending to single persons in our world when it has Sunday school classes labeled "Pairs and Spares"? The Dominion of God, according to Jesus, is a place where both fidelity in marriage and celibacy in singleness are valid callings for a Christian life (see Matthew 19 and 1 Corinthians 7). God's Dominion manifests itself when each person is affirmed as being of sacred worth, whether single or married, whether young or old, whether healthy or infirm, whether born or about to be born.

Finally, we need to say something about the difference between a church that recognizes the Dominion of God and one that has a Kingdom mentality. The Kingdom mentality manifests itself in arrogant pronouncements that the church is the one sole dispenser of God's grace and that its leaders should be treated as if their authority and decisions are unquestionable. By contrast a church that manifests the Dominion of God recognizes that only God is God and that the church's leaders are servants of God, not saviors. A church that manifests the Dominion of God does not indulge or encourage the cult of personality we sometimes find in churches, especially some megachurches. A minister who recognizes God's rule and saving work in the midst of the people will not think he or she is indispensable to the church. Rather, as a servant of God, he or she will seek to enable the gifts and graces of the church members, not disable them by trying to do or control all the church's ministries.

Jesus had very specific advice to his disciples about how they should lead and so make clear that only God rules and saves: "The kings of the Gentiles lord it over them; and those in authority over them are called benefactors. But not so with you. Rather the greatest among you must become like the youngest and the leader like one who serves. For who is greater, the one who is at the table or the one who serves? Is it not the one who is at the table? But I am among you as one who serves" (Luke 22:25-27). Leaders who model themselves on Christ's leadership style do not assume the position of the church's Lord, but rather the posture the church's Lord assumed when he was on earth, namely the form of a servant. This posture helps prevent the development of the Kingdom mentality in either the pastor or the parishioners.

We have sought in this chapter to discuss the location of God's Dominion on earth. We have stressed that God's Dominion cannot be confined to the context of the gathering of God's people, but that it may be found preeminently there. God's Dominion as it now exists refers to God's saving activity among human beings, which manifests itself in corporate worship and indeed also in a wide variety of works of charity and piety, including the sharing of the gospel and work for justice in human relationships and society. In the next chapter we must become more personal and ask how the Dominion manifests itself in an individual's life.

Questions for Reflection and Discussion

- In what sense is the Dominion of God "hiding in plain sight" in the present time?

- Where can it be said that God's Dominion is to be found on earth?

- Can the church be simply equated with God's Dominion?

- What are the qualities one looks for in a church that manifests the presence of God's Dominion?

- List several aspects of the church's worship, service, and practice that make evident that God's saving presence is at work in its midst.

- What is the difference between the Kingdom mentality and the recognition of God's Dominion in the church's life?

- What is the model for church leaders that is consistent with a recognition that God's Dominion is present and that Christ is the church's Lord?

CHAPTER THREE

Taking the Presence Personally

It is easy enough to talk about God's reign in the abstract, or even about how it manifests itself in the world or in the church, but what sort of inventory is required to discern how the Dominion of God, or the lordship of Christ, is present in an individual's life? How do we discern whether God's rule is spreading throughout a particular human heart or mind? There are in fact several spiritual inventories or litmus tests that one can use to pursue this question, as we shall now see.

It will be remembered that Jesus at one point during his ministry said that unless a person receives the Dominion as or like a child, he or she will never enter the Dominion of God in the future (Mark 10:15). It is also reported that Jesus remarked that children should be allowed to come to him because "it is to such as these that the Dominion of God belongs" (v. 14). This whole discussion is remarkable in several regards. First, Jesus is responding to the disciples' speaking sternly to people who were bringing their children to Jesus for his blessing. The disciples' assumptions seem to have been that Jesus' teaching and an encounter with Jesus were for adults only. This assumption was not uncommon in antiquity. In early Judaism children were not sent off to study with famous rabbis or Jewish teachers. Jesus, however, insists that there is a place in God's Dominion for children, and that in fact even adults cannot enter that Dominion unless they take on certain childlike qualities.

The child in antiquity was never set up as a model of discipleship, at least not until Jesus came along.

What then does it mean to say that one cannot enter the Dominion unless one receives the Dominion here and now as a child? I suspect that in the first place Jesus had in mind the fact that children have no difficulty receiving gifts. Indeed, nearly everything children receive comes as a gift, not as something they have earned. Have you ever noticed how at Christmas children have no difficulty receiving gifts, without immediately wondering who they must repay?

An adult, on the other hand, often has difficulty or feels uncomfortable with receiving a gift from someone he or she has not also given a gift to. Why is this? I suspect it is in part because our society tells us repeatedly "you don't get something for nothing" or "you get what you earn or pay for." Our culture is fundamentally works-oriented, not grace-centered. We like to think of ourselves as those who need no help, but rather, given an opportunity, can get it for ourselves. We like to be independent. A child, on the other hand, knows very well that he or she is dependent on others. Children are under no delusion that they have all that they get because they have or must have earned it or that it comes as part of some sort of gift exchange, some sort of "you scratch my back, I'll scratch yours" reciprocity ritual. They know how to receive, and this includes knowing how to receive the Dominion, the saving rule of God in one's life.

One of my best friends grew up with a friend named Sandy. Sandy was a talented and sensitive young man, but his heart was not open to the Lord, in part because of what had happened to his baby sister. She had become very ill when she was five or six years old. She was taken to the hospital and the prognosis was quite grim. Yet this young girl had a strong faith in Jesus, and whenever Sandy came to see his sister she would ask him, "Have you met my Jesus?" "Have you seen him?" This ongoing testimony of a child was eventually to change Sandy's life, but not until after his sister had died in the hospital. Today Sandy is a priest, serving God in a monastery. His life bears witness to the meaning of "and a little child shall lead them." He was shown the way to receive God's Dominion by a child, who had absolute trust and faith in Jesus and was open to receiving whatever God would give, was open to the saving rule of God in her life.

This I think is an essential part of what Jesus had in mind when he said we must receive God's Dominion like a child. We must ask ourselves if we are prepared to be open to allowing God to be Lord of our lives, allowing God to set the agenda for what we will say and do, how we will behave, the path and career we will follow in life. Above all we must ask ourselves if we are prepared to give our unconditional loyalty to God and place our unconditional trust in him, just as God has poured out his unconditional love into our hearts through the Holy Spirit (Rom. 5:5).

Sometimes it is difficult to pinpoint why we seem reticent to surrender totally to God's will and rule for our lives. Sometimes, perhaps, it is because we do not totally trust what God will do with us, and it is difficult if not impossible to love someone totally that you do not totally trust. This is as true in a human relationship such as marriage as it is in one's relationship to God. If we find ourselves in this position, finding it difficult to surrender totally to the lordship of Christ, we can always pray for more faith and grace in our lives, but we can also take courage from the example of those who exhibit a childlike faith and acceptance of God's lordship in their lives, like Sandy's sister.

The second major thing to say about Jesus' words in Mark 10:14-15 is that Jesus suggests that children and those who are like them are the sort of folk one finds in God's Dominion, which is another way of saying that such places are obtained by grace, not by works. If we think we can work or worm our way into God's good graces, we are sadly mistaken. The Dominion of God must be received with childlike faith and trust. It cannot be earned or bargained for or bought. We must ask ourselves whether we have allowed the character of our culture to shape our vision of how we relate to the Dominion of God or are really prepared to grasp and accept the concept of grace, which is to say God's unmerited favor, the undeserved benefits God bestows, because that is the character of God. God's rule in our lives is consistent with his character, and God's character is perfectly revealed both in the fact that he so loved us that he cared enough to send the very best, his only Son, to save us and in the character of Jesus while he was among us.

If we ask a bit further about what our lives should look like if we are living under the reign of God and not the reign of self or world, we can turn to the character descriptions given for what a Christian ought to look like in texts like Galatians 5:16-26, 1 Corinthians 13, and Matthew 5–7. Sometimes we may be forgiven for thinking that the clearest evidence that we are living under God's reign is that we have various flashy spiritual gifts with which to glorify God and edify others. It is true that this is an evidence of God's work and rule in a person's life, but as John Wesley once said, the gifts of the Spirit must be normed by the fruit of the Spirit. Christian character, rather than talent or giftedness, is a clearer sign of the reign of God in a person's life.

Let us then explore what Galatians 5:22-26, 1 Corinthians 13, and Matthew 5–7 tell us about Christian character. First, all these texts make clear that love is at the heart of the matter. The clearest sign of God's rule in a person's life is that he or she is a loving human being, prepared to manifest the sort of self-sacrificial giving Jesus manifested when he was here on earth. One of the ways I like to check my own progress in grace, or, as it is sometimes called, sanctification, is to ask myself now and then, "Am I a more loving person today than I was this time a month ago or a year ago?" If God is working in our lives, if God's rule is extending to more and more areas of who we are, then we should be able to see progress in manifesting Christ-like qualities.

Whenever I examine Galatians 5:16-26 I am struck not just with the list of the fruit of the Spirit but also by the list of things to which that fruit is contrasted — sexual immorality, idolatry, enmities, strife, jealousy, anger, quarrels, factions, drunkenness. What strikes me about this list is that these are all forms of human behavior that divide people, that break up homes, that destroy relationships, that are forms of self-centered and self-seeking behavior. The clear sign of God's rule in a person's life is that he or she behaves in loving ways, in ways that make for peace, in ways that make for healthy and happy relationships.

Let us then consider the list of the fruit of God's Spirit — love, joy, peace, patience, kindness, generosity, faithfulness, gentleness, self-control. Notice that Paul does not speak of the fruits of the Spirit here but of the *fruit,* singular. Also this text is about what God produces in a human being's life by the Spirit, not about character or traits one has had since birth. In other words, when the Spirit rules in our lives, we should expect to see all these traits manifested, not just one of them. If we do not see all of them, then we know the areas we need to pray about, to ask God to help us grow in grace and let the Dominion advance in our lives.

All these aspects of the fruit are qualities that bring and bind people together, that make for lasting relationships, friendships, and marriages. They also depict the character of Christ. He is the one who brought love, joy, and peace. He was the one who was kind to the lost, generous to the poor and to the poor in Spirit, faithful to his word and to his disciples, gentle in the laying of his yoke of discipleship on others, and above all always in control of himself, even to the point that when he was tempted to do something that was not God's will he would remember to pray "nevertheless not my will but thine be done."

Similar things could be said of the description of love given in 1 Corinthians 13:4-8: "Love is patient, love is kind, love is not envious, boastful, arrogant, or rude. It does not insist on its own way; it is not irritable or resentful; it does not rejoice in wrongdoing, but rejoices in the truth. It bears all things, believes all things, hopes all things, endures all things. Love never ends." This has also often been said to be an apt description of the character of Christ, just as it is intended to be a benchmark by which we measure our progress in conforming to the image of Christ, so manifesting God's perfect rule in our lives. Just as Jesus perfectly manifested God's rule in his own life, this is likewise the goal of God's work and rule in ours, so that when others look at us, they see Jesus.

Sometimes Christianity is mistakenly assumed to be a religion that inculcates weakness rather than strength in people, that weakens human personality rather than encouraging strong personality. The blessed meek of Matthew 5:5 are assumed to be the weak, the humble to be the inferior. Yet the model of meekness and humility is Jesus himself! If there has been one person who walked this earth who was not weak, not even in the face of supernatural evil, it was Jesus. He did not back down even from the power of evil, even from the cross of Rome. Furthermore, if there has been one person on this earth who did not suffer from an inferiority complex, it was Jesus. If there has ever been one person who was sure of who he was and what he ought to do with his life, if there has ever been a confident person, it was Jesus.

It follows from this that if Christ is the example of humility, humility has nothing to do with feelings of low self-worth or with self-degrading or self-defiling deeds. Rather, as Philippians 2:4-11 makes clear, humility has to do with deliberately choosing to make sacrifices, deliberately being willing to step down and take a lower place in order to lift others up. This takes character strength, not character flaws or weakness. Just as it takes a person of strong character to walk away and not fight back when someone strikes them, so it takes a person of strong, not weak character, to willingly make sacrifices for others. This is the character of Christ, the character of love. This is the Dominion of God ruling in a human life. It leads to people becoming servants of others, not lording it over others, whether in the church or in the family or in friendships or in business relationships.

Matthew 5–7 has often been said to be the blueprint for a Christian's life of discipleship. It is also a good litmus test to tell whether the Dominion of God is working its will in our lives. It should be said from the outset that it is quite impossible to follow this blueprint if we are talking about merely human effort. What Jesus asks of us here is only possible if God's rule and God's grace are working powerfully in our lives.

Consider what Jesus asks of us. He asks us not to insult or berate others. He asks of us that if we have anything against someone else, before we go to worship or give our offerings to God, we be reconciled with our brother or sister whom we have something against or he or she against us. "Forgive us our trespasses as we forgive those who trespass against us." Shortly after the Civil War, in an Episcopal Church in Richmond, an extraordinary thing happened. It was communion Sunday, and in this church for many years it had been the practice of both white families and their slaves to take communion, but separately, with the slaves coming last. On this particular Sunday, when the minister announced the call to come forward and take communion, an older black man, a former slave, stood up with the white folks and began to go forward to the communion rail. The white folks all froze, except one elderly gray-bearded white gentleman in the back of the church who came forward, took the black man by the arm, and went up and took communion with him. That man was Robert E. Lee, and thereafter there was no separate communion in that church.

Jesus asks of us not merely not to commit acts of sexual infidelity and immorality, he asks us to quench any such thoughts we have of this sort. He asks of us not merely not to swear falsely but not to swear at all. Our word should be our bond, our yes should mean yes and our no mean no. He asks of us that we not resist an evildoer. If we are struck an insulting blow, then we turn the other cheek and accept another rather than retaliate. Jesus calls us to live nonviolent lives, to be proactive rather than reactive when bad things happen to us. Furthermore if someone takes something from us that they need, such as clothing, Jesus asks that we be prepared to give that person even more. "Give to everyone who begs from you, and do not refuse anyone who wants to borrow from you" (Matt. 5:42).

Jesus asks of us that we not merely love our friends and family but love our enemies, those who wish to do us harm. Love of enemies is said to be a Godlike quality. Wherever you see it, since it goes against every natural human instinct, you see the grace of God working. It is not a natural response but one that happens because of the supernatural rule of God in someone's life.

Corrie Ten Boom was once confronted by the need to forgive her enemies personally and directly. She and her family were placed in a prison camp during WWII and her sister Betsy was beaten to death before her very eyes by a Nazi death camp guard. As she lay dying, Betsy could see the anger and hatred in Corrie's eyes and said to her with her last breath, "No hate, Corrie, only love." Years later, after Corrie had been miraculously released from the death camp and was sharing the gospel in Europe, a man came up to her and said, "Miss Ten Boom, I have come to ask your forgiveness. I was that guard who caused the death of your sister, and I have made my peace with God, but I need your forgiveness as well if I am to be at peace." Corrie said that she would pray about it, but she was unable to offer forgiveness on that day. Some time later, having wrestled in prayer over this matter, Corrie called the man and forgave him. This was not a natural response, but it was the sort of act that showed that God's reign was present in her life.

Jesus also asks of us to give charitably, to pray meaningfully, to fast regularly, to save sparingly, and not to serve two masters — God and money. When money has dominion over a person's heart and mind it is a harsh taskmaster. Since money and possessions can never fill up the God-shaped vacuum in the human heart, there is never enough. It always falls short of satisfying. It is easy to see why Jesus might compare money to God. When one places one's total trust in one's assets, they become one's God. They rule that person's life. They dictate how that person acts, when that person spends his or her money, who that person gives to, whom that person associates with, and more. All these things should in fact be done on the prompting of God in one's life, not out of enlightened self-interest. Not surprisingly, immediately after speaking about money, Jesus speaks about worry.

Some of the least happy people I have ever met have been wealthy. They were always worried about protecting what they had, protecting their investments and the like. They lived on the basis of fear of what might happen to them rather than faith in God. The parable of the man who stored things away in barns but died before he was able to enjoy the benefits of all his hard work stands as a reminder of Jesus' point. Life is short, one should love much and live on the basis of trust in God, not in one's own resources. Only God can provide eternal security. It is a sign of the presence of God's reign in a person's life if he or she is generous and prepared to make financial sacrifices to further the cause of the Kingdom.

Toward the end of the Sermon on the Mount, Jesus speaks to the subject of self-deception about one's relationship with God (Matt. 7:21-23). The essence of what he says is that though one may give lip-service to the Lord or even speak mighty words or do mighty deeds in Jesus' name, if that person does not do the will of God he or she will not enter God's Dominion. Here Jesus appears to have in mind not primarily the nominal believer but those who exercise the gifts of God for their own glory or self-aggrandizement. Here again there is a salutary warning. Godly character rather than goodly gifts and talents is a better indicator of whether God is ruling in a person's life or not.

The final exhortation of the Sermon to be doers and not merely hearers of the Word of God reminds us that Jesus expects us to work out what God is working in us, to act on the basis of the inward renovations God is making in our lives. Words without deeds are empty, but equally deeds done for the wrong reasons and to the wrong ends and so not in accord with God's will also do not manifest God's Dominion in one's life.

All of the above discussion has prepared us to examine the issue of personal salvation and sanctification a little more closely. We should ask, Why has God saved me? Why has he set up his rule in my life? First, we may say without hesitation that God has not saved an individual simply so he or she may dwell eternally with God. Salvation is of course the bestowal of the gift of eternal life, but having such a condition or gift is not the sole aim of God's work in our lives. It has been said we have been saved to serve, which is quite true, but we can speak more comprehensively about having been saved so that we might more perfectly manifest the character of God on earth in our lives through both our worship and our service and our daily lives. As God is holy love, so we are also to be holy and loving.

Holiness does not mean having a holier than thou attitude about other persons. This danger exists among believing people and is warned against by Jesus, who says not to judge lest we be judged in the same fashion. Yet the issue in "judge not . . ." is not whether we should be discerning nor about how we evaluate human behavior, for we certainly should be discerning. The issue is that none of us is the one who decides another person's eternal destiny, nor can we read a person's heart and so must leave his or her fate in God's hands and attend to our own. But we do have a moral responsibility, if we see brothers or sisters go astray, to warn them in a loving manner about how they are imperiling their spiritual lives and potentially their places in God's final Dominion.

Holiness of heart and life means both the hallowing of all life great and small, seeing it all as a gift of a gracious God and therefore of sacred worth, and purity of heart and behavior. The commitment to ethical integrity is crucial, for we are called on to manifest the character of Christ to the world.

About a decade ago we saw various wristbands and the like with "W.W.J.D." on them. This serves as a reminder to ask before one acts: What Would Jesus Do? It is a very good question. In the nineteenth century a medical missionary in Aintab, Armenia, named Dr. Sheppard was brought a small man who was near death and enduring much suffering. Dr. Sheppard slowly ministered him back to health, but he also shared the gospel of Christ with the man. In due course the man became both well and a Christian. He returned to his own village and like many a new convert could hardly stop talking about Jesus. At one point an irritated listener responded to the small man: "Why should I believe you? You have never even seen this Jesus. On your own account of things he died over 1,500 years ago." Undaunted, the little man immediately responded: "To the contrary, I have seen Dr. Sheppard, and Christ lives in him. And furthermore, Christ now lives in me."

Holiness in its purest form means manifesting the life and lifestyle of Christ in one's own life, manifesting the purity and power of Christ in one's own life, manifesting the graciousness and humility of Christ in one's own life. Though of course holiness involves not doing a variety of sins and misdeeds, as the list of vices in Galatians 5 (see above) makes clear, holiness is not primarily about what we are not or what we don't do, but rather primarily about what we are and what we must do. Holiness, then, is not primarily about what we abstain from but rather about what we manifest, namely the reign of God in our lives.

Awareness of God's reign in one's life necessarily changes one's view of life, the world, and what is important in living in this world. For one thing, a person who lives under the reign of God does not view this life as the be-all and end-all of existence. Such a person does not go around saying things like "You only go around once in life, so grab all the gusto you can get." Rather a Christian is one who lives in the light of eternity, manifesting the perspective of eternity here on earth. A person who has eternal life can be free to give his or her life if necessary for the sake of God's Dominion. He or she does not have to clutch this earthly existence as if it is all there is to life.

Not only do Christians with a Kingdom perspective not have to hold on to physical life tightly, they also do not have to hold their resources tightly. They can, rather, trust God and give generously. The same applies to what and whom one loves. The Christian under God's reign has been freed to love graciously, to love in all directions, to love indiscriminately. One of my fellow New Testament scholars likes to say that Christian love is not like a heat-seeking missile, prompted by something inherently attractive in the target. Rather, Christian love gives to all and sundry because it is the right thing, the Christ-like thing, to do.

It may be asked at this point whether living a Christian life requires a countercultural lifestyle. The answer depends on how Christian the dominant culture one lives in is. In an increasingly secular and post-Christian culture like the United States, a countercultural approach becomes more and more necessary because the dominant culture no longer endorses essential Christian values. Countercultural Christianity can take many forms. It can involve economic boycotts of companies that peddle pornography, which degrades both women and the men who buy it. It can involve protesting a war because the gospel requires that we love our enemies. It can involve protesting and working constructively against the marginalizing of society's weakest members — the elderly, the infirm, the unborn, the poor. It can involve working to help others who have experienced calamity without waiting for the government to take care of them. I was struck, when I lived in northeastern Ohio, by the fact that after the devastation of a tornado that swept through the region the Amish immediately began to rebuild the destroyed barns and houses in their area, while most others, including non-Amish Christians, stood around wringing their hands, angry about the slow response of the government to the disaster. Countercultural Christianity doesn't wait for a secular government to show compassion. It knows it must act on its own.

I have suggested that a countercultural lifestyle for the church under God's rule is becoming increasingly necessary. This means that the church must recover or do a better job with many responsibilities that during earlier ages it took as part of its mission — caring for the elderly and the marginalized, building homes (Habitat for Humanity), and working for the transformation of societal values. This, too, is part of what it means to manifest God's reign on the earth. Personal sanctification is necessary, but since Christians are called to live not in isolation but rather in community, the social dimension to holiness must be taken seriously. Christ's character must be manifest not just by individual Christians but by the body of Christ. Only so will the Dominion of God be seen to be coming on this earth.

In the first half of this study we have been concentrating on the present dimension of God's Dominion on earth. Yet it would be myopic if we stopped with such a discussion, for there are at least as many passages in the New Testament that focus on the future manifestation of God's Dominion on earth. What will it be like when that future Dominion breaks into human history? Where will it be found and how may we prepare for its coming? These are some of the issues we must address in the second half of this study.

Questions for Reflection and Discussion

- ☞ What did Jesus mean by saying that one must receive God's reign like a child?

- ☞ What attributes of a child do you think Jesus wanted his disciples to emulate?

- ☞ What is the difference between a simple faith and an immature faith?

- ☞ What are the fruit of the Spirit, and how do they affect human relationships?

- ☞ Is having a Christ-like character possible? In what sense?

- ☞ It has been suggested that one should have a regular spiritual check-up to see how one is growing in grace. What sort of questions should one be asking?

- ☞ What does the term "holiness" mean?

- ☞ What is the character of Christian love?

- ☞ What does the term "grace" mean?

- ☞ How is holiness different from being holier than thou?

- ☞ When might a countercultural lifestyle be required of a Christian?

PART TWO

THE GLORIOUS FUTURE

CHAPTER FOUR

"Thy Kingdom Come"

In some ways it is easier to talk about the Dominion of God in the present, but harder to visualize it. It is easier to talk about because we live in an experiential age, an age quite prepared to talk about life-transforming events or encounters. Yet on the other hand it is easier to envision the future of God's Dominion, easier to come up with potent images of what it will look like ("the lion will lie down with the lamb," "swords will be beaten into plowshares"), yet harder for many to relate to or believe in. Even some Christians would be prepared to say that after 2,000 long years Jesus is probably not coming back to bring human history to a climax.

In part the loss of a viable hope for the future of the world and replacement of it with a dying and going to heaven sort of hope, an other-worldly hope, is understandable. Yet this failure of nerve and of faith is not justifiable, and often it is grounded in a misunderstanding of what the New Testament actually says about the future of God's Dominion.[1]

Three things need to be stressed at this point: (1) The New Testament says nothing explicit about the timing of the second coming of

---

1. On this entire subject see my *Jesus, Paul, and the End of the World* (Downers Grove: InterVarsity, 1992). On proper Christian hope in regard to the future see now N. T. Wright, *Surprised by Hope* (San Francisco: Harper One, 2008).

47

Christ, but simply affirms the fact of that coming. Indeed, Mark 13:32 informs us that Jesus himself said during his ministry that he did not know the timing of the second coming of the Son of Man. (2) Often when the issue of timing comes up we fail to bear in mind that God is not a creature bound within the space-time universe. God transcends time and is not limited by time as we know it within the material universe. This is in part what is meant in 2 Peter 3:8-10: "With the Lord one day is like a thousand years, and a thousand years are like one day. The Lord is not slow about his promise . . . but is patient with you, not wanting any to perish, but all to come to repentance. But the day of the Lord will come like a thief. . . ." (3) The earliest Christians, since they did not know the timing of Christ's return, were prepared to reckon with and hope for the possibility that Christ would return in their own day, but they used images like the thief in the night to convey the fact that Christ would come at a surprising or unexpected time and therefore that one must always be ready. The upshot of all this is that it is a mistake to suggest that the earliest Christians believed that Christ would definitely return in their own age and then, when that proved untrue, had to conjure with the delay of the Royal Return. The viable future of God's Dominion on earth should not be dismissed on the basis of a misreading of what the New Testament claims about the timing of Christ's return.

The Lord's Prayer, which the church today should and must pray in good faith, includes the words "Thy Kingdom come, thy will be done, on earth as in heaven." This prayer makes it clear that God's Dominion in heaven is not the same as God's future Dominion on earth, or otherwise there would be no point to this petition. The petition suggests that the Dominion is not yet fully present on earth as it already is in heaven. Bearing these things in mind, a series of questions need to be considered at this point.

Let us consider first the meaning of the term "heaven." Heaven is the dwelling place of God. Since God is thought to be omnipresent, some have reasoned that therefore heaven is likewise everywhere. This represents a misunderstanding of the concept of God's omnipresence. The Bible does not affirm that a little bit of God is everywhere or in all things in the material universe. This notion has rightly been dubbed pantheism. The God of the Bible is not a substance or a force that permeates all things. He is a personal being, indeed a tri-personal being, one who is Father, Son, and Spirit. When the Bible speaks of God being present everywhere, what is actually meant is that all things are present to God at once, for God is much greater than, far more enormous than, the material universe. God is not an item within that universe but the Maker of it. "He's got the whole world in his hands. . . ."

So when we speak of heaven, we are not speaking of a place within the material universe, say just outside the earth's atmosphere. We are speaking of the eternal dwelling place of God, from which God created the whole universe. Furthermore, God can be distinguished from heaven. For instance, God can be near, or in our midst, and heaven still be remote. This means that while God in the person of the Holy Spirit is dwelling within God's people, nonetheless heaven does not now exist on earth. But when we discuss the future of God's Dominion the idea is that there will be, as it were, a merger of heaven and earth. God will make his final and eternal dwelling place with those who dwell below. At that point, heaven will come down and earth will be transformed.

Another clear sign that heaven is not envisioned as being here on earth in the present is that the New Testament speaks of believers dying and going to heaven. The famous parable of the rich man and Lazarus makes this point very clearly (Luke 16:19-31). What is not usually noticed by many modern readers of the New Testament is that heaven is not envisioned as the final dwelling place of God's people. "Resurrection of the dead" is the language the New Testament uses over and over again to speak of the final future of God's people, and this has to do not with life in heaven but rather with life in a new embodied condition on earth. The ultimate future of humankind is not in a disembodied existence somewhere outside the material universe but rather in a resurrection body here in space and time. We need to put some flesh on some of these bare bones ideas by examining a variety of texts.

Let us deal with the issue of the endtimes in general first. The Apostles' Creed, which the church has affirmed for centuries, includes these words: "I believe in Jesus Christ who . . . on the third day rose from the dead, ascended into heaven, and sits at the right hand of God, from whence he will come to judge the living and the dead. . . . I believe in . . . the resurrection of the body and the life everlasting." Now lest we think this creedal statement is merely redundant, the second reference to resurrection refers not to Jesus' resurrection, like the first, but to the future resurrection of believers. This is not a novel doctrine but something the church has always affirmed as part of its faith. It is important also to stress that the resurrection of the dead is contingent on the return of Christ. The former will not happen unless or until the latter happens.

Indeed, one can say that the whole schedule of eschatological events hinges on the return of Christ. Until and unless Christ returns, there will be no resurrection of the dead, no final judgment, no life everlasting, no Dominion of God on earth as in heaven. In many ways the return of Christ is a trigger event much like the resurrection of Christ was. As Paul puts it in 1 Corinthians 15, if Christ is not raised, then the dead are not raised. If Christ is not raised, then our faith is in vain, we are still in our sins. As with so many things in Christian theology, an understanding of the whole career of Christ, both past and future, leads to an understanding of our future and the future of God's Dominion. Indeed, as we shall see, Christ's history is our destiny.

Human beings are time- and space-bound creatures. The creation story itself in Genesis 1–2 makes evident that we could not fully exist without an embodied condition, without a supportive material environment in which to live, complete with air, water, food, and much more. The propagation and preservation of the human species likewise depends on not just one type of embodied existence but rather two types — male and female.

When the New Testament speaks of the new creation it means exactly that — a renewal or transformation or re-creation of the creation that already exists. The end times are envisioned as being like and yet superior to the beginning times for the human race. It is thus a mistake to assume that the New Testament writers envisioned dying and going to heaven as the final condition of human beings. Rather, that was seen as a blessed interim condition on the way to the new heaven and the new earth. Even the martyred saints under the altar in heaven are not satisfied: they ask "How long?" (Rev. 6:9-10). The new creation began during Jesus' ministry, reached its first climactic point with the resurrection of Jesus, and will not be completed until Christ comes again.

One of the most crucial texts in the New Testament for this topic and the basis of a good deal of the church's creedal statements about the future is 1 Corinthians 15. This text, especially certain key verses, provides crucial material for the church's proclamation at Easter. We are all likely familiar with "Christ died for our sins in accordance with the Scriptures, and . . . he was buried, and . . . he was raised on the third day in accordance with the Scriptures, and . . . he appeared to Cephas, then to the Twelve, then he appeared to more than 500 brothers and sisters" (15:3-6). But it is in this same chapter that Paul provides a brief sketch of the future. After referring to Christ as the firstfruits of the resurrection from the dead, he says, "then at his coming those who belong to Christ. Then comes the end, when he hands the Dominion to God the Father after he has destroyed every ruler and every authority and power. For he must reign until he puts all his enemies under his feet. The last enemy to be destroyed is death. . . . When all things are subjected to him, then the Son himself will also be subjected to the One who put all things in subjection under him, so that God may be all in all" (15:23-28).

Lest we think that Paul means something different when he refers to the resurrection of believers than he meant when referring to Christ's resurrection, consider verses 50-54: "flesh and blood," that is, physical life as it now exists, "cannot inherit the Dominion of God, nor does the perishable inherit the imperishable. . . . We will not all die, but we will all be changed, in a moment, in the twinkling of an eye, at the last trumpet. For the trumpet will sound, and the dead will be raised imperishable, and we will be changed. For this perishable body must put on imperishability, and this mortal body must put on immortality." Paul links the resurrection of Christ to the resurrection of those in Christ with the metaphor about the first and the latter fruits, and he makes clear that the believer's future will be like Christ's past — in each case ending in an embodied state, the resurrection body, which is immune to disease, decay, and death. Resurrection is something that happens to dead persons, but Paul also affirms that there will be believers alive on earth when Christ returns and they will be changed or transformed into a resurrection state.

Notice that when Paul speaks of this final future for believers he refers twice also to the Dominion of God. He says emphatically that believers in their current mortal state cannot participate in the final form of the Dominion of God. To participate in the imperishable new creation, one must be in an imperishable condition, and more particularly one must have a resurrection body like Christ's. Then, when Christ has accomplished what God sends him to do at and after the second coming, namely set up the final form of God's rule on earth, he will return the Dominion of God to the Father, who will reign over all forever. The Dominion of God in both future salvation and future judgment is closely linked to what Christ will yet do when he returns. The goal of God is not merely to reign in or from heaven, but to reign upon the earth forever. In God's plan, creation, like human creatures, has a future, not least because God cares about all that he has made.

The important point to be made about all this is that if one can believe that God raised Christ from the realm of the dead 2,000 years ago, in principle there should be no difficulty with the concept of the resurrection of believers in the future. The timing of the event is surely a secondary issue compared to the possibility of the event. Notice, too, that the completion of the Dominion of God does not come when believers die and go to heaven, but rather when God's full reign, even over death, becomes a reality, becomes evident on earth. When we pray "Thy Kingdom come, thy will be done" we are praying for the return of Christ, the resurrection of the dead, the last judgment, and the life to come, in which the Dominion is finally fully manifested on earth.

It is of course true that God's Dominion, his perfect reign, is already happening in heaven, but this should not lead us to equate heaven and God's Dominion. Heaven is currently a place, God's Dominion is the condition of that place, and is in part the condition of the life of believers on earth. We are in various respects the manifestation of the reality of the Dominion on earth here and now. The Dominion, then, or God's saving reign, involves both heaven and earth and one day will encompass both heaven and earth.

What we have said thus far in this chapter should make it clear that there has been, is, and will be a historical dimension or expression of God's Dominion. God is not content simply to reign in heaven. Indeed the whole of the New Testament is about God so loving the world that he sent his Son to establish that Dominion on earth, as in heaven. This necessarily means that Christians can never afford to devalue either creation or its future, whether that bit of creation known as our bodies or the rest of creation, both animate and inanimate. It is never an adequate theology to say "this world is not my home, I'm just passing through" as if heaven were all that really mattered. To the contrary, the New Testament suggests just the opposite. Heaven is not the believer's home. It is simply a place through which they pass between the time they die and when they are raised from the dead.

Of course it is true, as Paul says, that "to be absent from the body is to be present with the Lord" (2 Cor. 5:8). It is also often true that life in heaven is preferable to suffering and sorrow, pain and dying, on the earth (Phil. 1:20-25). But there are three states that need to be compared: life here on earth in the flesh, life in heaven, and life in the resurrection body in the world to come. Paul unequivocally states that he would prefer to live on this earth until the resurrection and simply be "further clothed" with a resurrection body rather than die (2 Cor. 5:4-5). The state of ultimate bliss is life on earth in the resurrection body. It is no accident that the historic ritual of the church for funerals contains primarily the proclamation of the hope of resurrection rather than the hope of life without a body in heaven. It is resurrection that is a death-defying event. It is resurrection that makes clear that God is Lord not only of life but also of death. It is resurrection that makes evident that God's yes to life is louder than death's no. It is resurrection that makes clear that God will rule on earth as it is in heaven. It is resurrection that makes God's Dominion on earth not just a hope but a reality.

It is at this point that something must be said about Christianity as a historical religion. Our faith is in part based on and grounded in God's track record, what God has already accomplished in space and time. It is not simply faith in faith, or wishful thinking about the future. We believe that as God has already once raised Jesus from the dead, he can perform such a miracle again for those who love him. Christ's history, his own real life story, is the basis for our hope that God's Dominion will one day come fully on the earth. Ours is not a religion based on a philosophy of life. It is based on certain irreducible facts of history, in particular the death and resurrection of Christ. If Christ was not raised, there is no point in talking about the future of God's Dominion on earth. If there has been and will be no resurrection, then there will be no "Kingdom come" here below in any full sense. If this is true, then Christianity indeed can at best only resign itself to an other-worldly hope for the future, for we cannot expect God to be sovereign here below over the forces of darkness, disease, decay, and death.

I have been stressing that the balance of the New Testament witness emphasizes the historical character and locale of God's Dominion.

God's intent is to rule in this world, not just in heaven. That is what God's interventions in human history, God's acts of salvation, are all about. To speak only of God's Dominion in heaven is to give up God's claim on creation. Believers are God's beachhead on earth in a lost world, but God is not content to reign only in the lives of believers. He is the God of heaven and all the earth. We can say then that the New Testament stresses that God's Dominion will only fully come on earth through further incursions in human history, particularly at the end through the second coming of Christ.

Bearing all this in mind, we need now to say something about end-time prophecy and the like. To judge from the supermarket tabloids, the passing of the year 2000 has done nothing to discourage end-time forecasting. With all the hype and hysteria, three facts need to be kept in mind: (1) Jesus was born somewhere between 6 and 4 B.C. Therefore, the year 2000 had no special import for biblical prophecy, for we passed the 2000-year mark from the time of Christ's birth several years before then! (2) All previous predictions about the timing of the return of Christ have one thing in common: they have all been 100 percent wrong. Earnestness and fervor about the timing of the final events of human history does not equal knowledge about such things. (3) The New Testament says a lot about the end times, but does not specify the timing of the end. The fact or reality of what is to come should not be dismissed or discredited on the basis of unbiblical speculation about the timing of such events.

One passage that has been subject to all sorts of misunderstanding and deserves close attention is 1 Thessalonians 4:13–5:11. On the basis of this passage it has been thought: (1) that Paul affirmed that Christ would definitely return in his own lifetime, that therefore Paul was wrong, and that we can dismiss all of what Paul says about the future of God's Dominion since he got the timing wrong, and (2) that Paul affirmed the rapture of the church prior to the final tribulation and the return of Christ.

In regard to the first of these claims I would want to stress that Paul uses the thief in the night metaphor in 1 Thessalonians 5:1-11 to make clear both that no one knows the timing of Christ's return and that the believer should not be caught by surprise in regard to the fact of the event. Since Paul did not know the timing of either the return of Christ or his own death, he considered it possible (not certain) that Christ might return during his lifetime. Thus when he says "we who are alive, who are left when the Lord returns," it must be remembered that with the two unknowns he had to conjure with there was no category to place himself in other than the living. He could not have said, for instance, "we who will die before the Lord returns" because he did not know the timing of either of these events. In short, this text does not by any means prove that Paul was convinced that Christ would necessarily have to come during his own lifetime.

As for the ever popular issue of the "rapture," it needs to be recognized that this theology did not arise before the nineteenth century as part of what was called dispensationalism and was popularized through the Scofield Reference Bible. There is no historical evidence that the early church believed in such a concept. To the contrary, the early church took texts like Mark 13:20 to mean that the church would go through the final tribulation while awaiting the second coming of Christ.

In 1 Thessalonians 4:16-17 Paul is using familiar imagery of a greeting committee going out to meet a returning king and to welcome him into the city. It is much like the entrance liturgy we find in Psalm 24:7-10. As the king and his entourage return to the city, the herald goes before the king and blows the trumpet to alert those on the city walls that the king has arrived and should be properly welcomed. Then the greeting committee goes to meet the king outside the city walls and he and those with him are ushered into the city.

Paul seems to leave us hanging with "then we who are alive will be caught up in the clouds together with the risen to meet the Lord in the air, and so we will be with the Lord forever" (1 Thess. 4:17). He does not say where believers will go once they meet the Lord in the air. But the larger context provides the clues. Paul does not say that believers will be taken up into heaven. Instead, they will be caught up into the clouds to meet the returning Christ. Paul is not here affirming the presence of clouds in heaven! But Paul's converts in Thessalonike would be likely familiar with his imagery of a royal return since they knew very well of the history of Philip and Alexander, the kings of Macedon. We may assume that they would have deduced that once the believers meet the Lord, they will all return with him to earth, where they will finish bringing in God's Dominion. If this is correct, there is certainly no rapture theology here. This text, like all these other texts, must be interpreted in terms of what the first audience was likely to understand them to mean, not in light of later Christian theological schemas of which the early Christians were ignorant.

Our study in this chapter has ranged through a variety of important topics having to do with the future coming of God's Dominion. We have dealt with both the fact and the timing of such an event. Perhaps the most important thing I can say about that future coming is that it is in God's hands. That is why we pray for it to come on earth rather than simply bringing it about ourselves. In particular, it is in the hands of the returning Christ, who will bring it about both by overruling the powers of darkness on earth and by raising the dead and judging both the living and the dead. This is the process by which God's will, including both justice and mercy, will finally be done on earth as in heaven. This is not a human self-help program but rather a divine activity and program. We will say more along these lines and about the implications of all this in the next chapter.

Questions for Reflection and Discussion

☞ What are some of the misunderstandings people have today about the future coming of God's Dominion, the future coming of Christ, or the future resurrection of believers?

☞ Where is heaven, and what is it?

☞ What is the difference between heaven and the Dominion of God?

☞ Why do we pray for God's Dominion to come, and what are we asking for when we do so?

☞ Why do you think the modern church has focused so much on the afterlife rather than the life to come on earth when Christ returns?

☞ Does the New Testament specify when Christ will return, or does it simply give an outline of what will happen when he does so?

☞ What is the relationship between resurrection and God's Dominion?

☞ What would it mean for human civilization as we know it if Christ came again to judge the living and the dead?

CHAPTER FIVE

"Thy Will Be Done"

We have spoken in a very general way about the eschatological future, including the future of God's Dominion, in the previous chapter. Some of the texts we have discussed have suggested that not everyone will be included in God's final Dominion. For example, you will remember Jesus' warning that some that expect to be in God's Dominion when it comes in fullness will be left out (Luke 13:28-30). To this we could add the more subtle point that Paul suggests that only those belonging to Christ will receive a resurrection body like Christ's (see 1 Cor. 15:23). We may also wish to reflect on even more ominous texts like Matthew 13:41-42: "The Son of Man will send his angels, and they will collect out of his Dominion all causes of sin and all evildoers, and they will throw them into the furnace of fire. . . . Then the righteous will shine like the sun in the Dominion of their Father." We could also point to parables like the one about the separation of the sheep and the goats (Matt. 25:31-46), which concludes with "And these will go away into eternal punishment, but the righteous into eternal life," or the parable of the wise and foolish bridesmaids (Matt. 25:1-13). There is no need to belabor the point. Suffice it to say that the cumulative impression of these texts is clear: not everyone will be saved, even though God desires that no one perish. It has been said that hell is the place where God says to the obstinate and hardhearted, "Thy will be done."

Precisely because the consistent witness of the New Testament is that some have rejected the gospel, will continue to do so, and will be ultimately lost, this raises in an acute form the issue of final salvation for those outside Christ, for Israel, and indeed for some who are church members but perhaps not true believers. Furthermore, one may wish to ask, if in the end not all are included in God's Dominion, what will be the extent of that Dominion? Where else could one be if God's Dominion will extend throughout the earth? These are difficult and delicate questions, but they must be raised and discussed if we are to gain clarity about the nature and future of God's saving reign on the earth.

Perhaps the place to begin is to remind ourselves that these subjects must be approached with humility and candor, not with arrogance and a judgmental attitude, especially since anyone who is still alive is still within the reach of God's grace and Good News. There is no justification in the New Testament for writing off any living soul or any group of people.

From there we should move to the thorny issue of anti-Semitism, because it is sometimes charged that the New Testament, especially Matthew's Gospel, John's Gospel, and some of Paul's letters, manifest anti-Semitic ideas.

This is in many ways an odd charge, not least because Paul was a Jew, as were, it would appear, the authors of Matthew and John. It would be nearer to the mark to say that various New Testament authors engage in what amounts to an in-house or prophetic critique of the religion of which they were a part. It will be remembered that the Old Testament prophets were often very strong critics of their own people and their religious practices, and yet no one today would accuse them of anti-Semitism. What is being criticized in the New Testament is a particular form of early Judaism, not Jews as an ethnic group nor Israel as a nation. The object of critique is especially Jews that rejected the notion of Jesus as the Jewish Messiah and the Savior of the world. In the view of the New Testament writers, true Judaism necessarily included the recognition of Jesus as the Messiah.[1] For example, Paul's vision of God's people in the new age is Jew and Gentile, slave and free, male and female, all united in Christ (Gal. 3:28).

Paul above all New Testament writers agonized over the issue of the future of Israel, especially when he saw the majority of his fellow Jews rejecting the gospel. Yet it needs to be stressed that even this repeated rejection did not stop Paul from sharing the gospel in the synagogue repeatedly (see Acts 13ff.) even at the cost of being punished severely several times for doing so (2 Cor. 11:24). This repeated rejection of Paul's gospel also did not cause him to offer a final anathema and stop praying for or thinking about his people. He even says that he would be prepared to give up his own salvation in Christ for the sake of his people (Rom. 9:3).

Romans 9–11 is an impassioned plea to the largely Gentile congregations of Roman Christians to recognize that God was not finished with his first chosen people, the Jews. Listen to what Paul says about these non-Christian Jews in Romans 9:4-5: "They are Israelites, and to them belong the adoption, the glory, the covenants, the giving of the law, the worship, and the promises; to them belong the patriarchs, and from them, according to the flesh, comes the Messiah. . . ." For Paul, the whole matter comes down to whether God is as good as his word, good as his promises or not. God's own character is at stake in Paul's view, for if God made many promises to the Jews, some of them apparently unconditional, and then turned around and reneged on those promises,

---

1. I would thus suggest that even the prevalent argument that what we find in the New Testament is anti-Judaism (a rejection of early Jewish religion) rather than anti-Semitism (a form of racism) is also not specific enough. It is not every aspect of early Jewish religion that is being critiqued by the New Testament writers. For example, none of them argue that the Hebrew Scriptures are not God's Word, that those Scriptures do not require a monotheistic faith, or that Abraham was not the forefather of God's chosen people. The critique found in the New Testament does not amount to a whole-scale rejection of early Judaism. What it really amounts to is a rejection of the prior rejection of the gospel and its implications by various Jews.

on what basis could Gentiles or anyone else trust such a capricious God? This is a very good question indeed and one that Paul struggles to provide an answer for at length in Romans 9–11.

It is not possible to work through all the complexities of Paul's argument here, but four key points can be made. First, Paul does indeed believe that Jesus is the Jewish Messiah, which also means that he believes God's promises for Jews are and will be fulfilled — but in Christ and not apart from Christ. This point is made very clear in 2 Corinthians 1:20: "For in Christ every one of God's promises is a 'Yes.' For this reason it is through him that we say the 'Amen' to the glory of God."

Second, Paul says very pointedly to the Gentile Christians in Rome that God was not caught by surprise when various Jews rejected the Good News about Jesus Christ. Because of this rejection, Paul says, these Jews have been temporarily broken off from the people of God (he uses the analogy of an olive tree and its branches: Rom. 11:17-22). And he stresses that Jews can be grafted back in if they do not persist in their unbelief (vv. 23-24).

Third, Paul believes that various Jews will be grafted back into God's people when Christ returns and the dead are raised. He says this in a variety of ways. In Romans 11:12 Paul speaks of the Jews' eventual full inclusion in Christ. In 11:15 he calls their acceptance of Christ equivalent to "life from the dead," a possible allusion to the resurrection. In 11:29 he reminds his audience that the gifts given to Israel and the call of Israel are irrevocable. In the conclusion of his argument he even says that when Christ returns "all Israel will be saved" (v. 26), by which he means a very large number. "The Deliverer will banish ungodliness from Jacob" and "take away their sins" (11:26-27), and they will be saved on the same basis as Gentiles are — by grace through faith in Christ.

Fourth, it becomes clear on a close reading of this entire argument in Romans 9–11 that Paul believes that a sovereign God has in fact broken off some natural olive branches (Jews) from God's people in order to go ahead in the present and graft wild olive branches (Gentiles) into

God's people by grace through faith. Yet God also broke off these Jews in order to have mercy on them as well, so that they might rejoin the people of God on the basis of grace and faith, rather than on the basis of assumed inheritance rights and the like.

What are the implications of this astounding argument? It means quite clearly that Christians at no point should write Jews off as eternally lost or damned. Nor is it even historically accurate to accuse Jews of having crucified Jesus. The occupying Romans executed Jesus, though a distinct minority of Jews, some of the Jewish leaders, had a hand in applying pressure to Pontius Pilate to carry out this deed. Paul reminds us repeatedly that the final chapter in the story of God's Dominion on earth has not yet been written and that when it is written there will be many saved Jews and Gentiles in that Dominion.

I would suggest that precisely because of this open-ended way of viewing the future of Israel, we must be careful how we speak about discussions today between Jews and Christians. Though on the one hand it is clear that we must describe talks between Jews and Christians today as interfaith dialogue (not ecumenical discussion, which implies two parties that affirm essentially the very same religion), yet it is not interfaith dialogue of the same ilk as, for instance, talks between Christians and Buddhists. Jews and Christians share a common scriptural heritage and to an important extent a common religious heritage. What we especially disagree about at this point is the means of salvation and Jesus' role in that process. There will be and necessarily are things about which we will have to continue to disagree respectfully with one another, for example, whether the New Testament can be considered part of Holy Scripture or whether Jews must believe in Jesus to be saved. But at no point have Christians any right to say or suggest that God has forsaken the Jews or closed the book on them. Christianity should not be seen as the religion that superseded Judaism. To the contrary, Paul saw the faith that he called and proclaimed as the Good News as the legitimate and necessary develop-

ment of the Jewish faith into its proper messianic and final eschatological form.

What are the implications of this discussion for other forms of interfaith dialogue? Here we must say that anyone who believes in a God
of love, a God who desires that no one should perish, must be open to
interfaith dialogue and approach such conversations with humility. Yet
a frank recognition of essential differences at the end of such discussions is not only likely, but in fact regularly happens, unless one or the
other party is prepared to give up the distinctives of their religion. For
example, if a group of Muslims were to affirm the Bible as God's Word
and reject the Koran, or at least reject its distinctive interpretations of
the Bible, of Judaism, and Christianity, then we might begin to have ecumenical discussions with such a group. Even if this never happened,
there are important issues of peace, justice, and love about which Christians should be able to make common cause with peoples of other reli-
gions. Whether it is Habitat for Humanity or some of the work of the
United Way or Bread for the World, there are many good causes worth
supporting that are consistent with and a legitimate extension of the
gospel and deserve our assistance.

Yet even if such a miraculous acceptance of the gospel by Muslims
or others did not happen on some occasion, much would still be gained
by understanding what our differences are and probing to see where areas of agreement, whether little or large, might be found. It is my view
that the essential differences between Judaism and Christianity are less
numerous and severe than between Christianity and any other world
religion, not least because early Christianity was in many respects an
offshoot from early Judaism. There is indeed a wideness in God's mercy,
and the Good News is open for all to respond, but God did not promise
salvation in advance to all and sundry. Yet we must bear in mind that
there are no promises in Scripture that a non-Christian group other
than non-Christian Jews will in some inevitable way be included in the
final form of God's people.

Sometimes when people are discussing the issues being addressed in this chapter, they speak of the "scandal of particularity." By this they suggest that anyone who proclaims their religion as the only means of salvation is arrogant and ignorant, and is guilty of unjustifiable religious chauvinism. I do not personally think that the scandal of particularity found in the New Testament can, or for that matter should be, overcome. The New Testament is unequivocal that Jesus Christ is God's chosen means of salvation. Yet it is important to remember that there is a potential universalism within Christian particularity. All may be saved through and in Christ, though the evidence is clear enough that many have chosen not to avail themselves of this opportunity.

The issues here are complex. For example, is it possible for God to reveal the divine nature and plan in some definitive way in a particular holy book? Historically and today the vast majority of Jews, Christians, and for that matter Muslims have all answered this question with an emphatic yes. God is capable of accurately and adequately revealing his will and divine plan of salvation. Yet there are many today who do not view any holy book as really a revelation from God, but rather see it as a human book which reflects the gropings of humankind after God, a series of inadequate attempts by humans to formulate their own faith. This view of course flatly contradicts texts like 2 Timothy 3:16: "All Scripture [in this case the Old Testament is meant] is God-breathed and is useful for teaching. . . ."

If the concept of a sovereign God's ability to reveal the divine plan in an accurate and adequate way to a group of people is granted, then the question becomes whether we have a right to tell God how the plan must work or to suggest that God really did not mean what the Word says God meant. I suggest that we have no such right. A Christian is a person under the authority of God's Word, not over that Word as some final arbiter of truth.

In my view, God is perfectly free to make up a plan for the salvation of humankind and execute it as he sees fit. He does not owe salvation to anyone, unless he first promised that salvation to some person or persons. We must remind ourselves that the New Testament says that all human beings have sinned and fallen short of God's best for us (Rom. 3:23). Salvation, then, becomes not a matter of something owed to us, but rather a gift of God's unfailing grace. This means that whether or not everyone is saved is not a issue of justice or of God's character. Rather, it is an issue of human character and human responsibility. While it is true that many today would like to live in a no-fault world, the New Testament is quite clear about human beings' moral responsibility for their actions, including responsibility for responding to the gospel.

This entire approach to the issue of salvation inevitably leads to the question — What about those who have not heard the gospel? Are they eternally lost just because they have not heard? The answer to this question must be no. If the answer were yes, then indeed there would be an issue about the character of God and whether we could take seriously Scripture's testimony that God is love and desires no one to perish.

Romans 1:18-32 deals with just this question. Paul is speaking of Gentiles who have not heard the gospel or for that matter heard the Hebrew Scriptures. Nevertheless, Paul says that "what can be known about God is plain to them, because God has shown it to them. Ever since the creation of the world God's eternal power and divine nature, invisible though they are, have been understood and seen through the things God has made" (vv. 19-20). Here Paul is suggesting that the reality and power of the one true God are revealed in creation and that since God has already made human beings in God's image they are capable of understanding this general revelation. The question is, how would they respond to this general revelation? Paul goes on to paint a rather bleak picture of repeated negative responses to general revelation.

The point, however, is that no one is condemned for what he or she does not know. All people are judged by what they do with the light they have received. Thus Paul is able to conclude that "they are without excuse; for though they knew God, they did not honor him as God or give thanks to him, but they became futile in their thinking, and their senseless minds were darkened" (vv. 20-21).

What, then, will be the scope of God's Dominion when the climax of history comes? The Scriptures suggest that ultimately God's Dominion will be coterminous with the entire world. Even in the Old Testament we hear promises like that found in Daniel 7, where it is said that the Son of Man will have an everlasting Dominion over the earth and that all peoples and nations will serve him (7:14). Yet even in the beautiful revelation of the new Jerusalem in Revelation 21, which speaks of God and heaven coming down and dwelling with humans on earth, we also find the reminder "But as for the cowardly, the faithless, the polluted, the murderers, the fornicators, the sorcerers, the idolaters, and all liars, their place will be in the lake that burns with fire and sulfur, which is the second death" (v. 8). Even allowing for dramatic hyperbole in the poetic description of the final state of affairs, the point is made clearly more than once that not all will be saved. When the new Jerusalem itself is described, it is stressed that "nothing unclean will enter it, nor anyone who practices abomination or falsehood, but only those who are written in the Lamb's book of life" (v. 27). This implies that some are inside the New Jerusalem and some outside.

What then should we make of the promise that every knee will eventually bow (whether on earth, in heaven, or under the earth), and every tongue confess that Jesus Christ is Lord, to the glory of God the Father (Phil. 2:10-11)? Here the point is to stress that in due course, when God makes it plain at the end of time and when Christ returns to rule the world, all will of necessity recognize Jesus for who he is. Like the demons in the Synoptic Gospels who regularly recognize Jesus for who he is but are not transformed by that truth (e.g., Mark 5:7), so, too, at the end all will have to acknowledge the truth about Christ whether willingly or unwillingly, whether wittingly or unwittingly. John Wesley once remarked that a person can be as orthodox as the Devil (by which he meant that the Devil knows the truth about Jesus Christ) and not benefit at all because he or she has not willingly received and been transformed by this truth. The final issue of salvation is not simply what people know but what they do with what they know of God. This is as true, as we have seen, in Paul's discussion in Romans 1 as in Philippians 2.

We have covered a great deal of ground in a short span of pages and it will be well if we sum up the implications of what has been said. First, we have stressed that though Christ's saving work is sufficient for all human beings in every generation it is only efficient or beneficial for those who appropriate it by faith. It is like a person depositing in a bank a million dollars and then telling the lucky beneficiary that it's there. Yet if the beneficiary does not draw on the account, indeed even refuses to, it will never benefit that person. The benefit does not happen automatically. Salvation is a matter of a personal relationship with God through Jesus Christ. It is not a benefit simply bestowed by God apart from any such relationship.

Second, this means we must take seriously the numerous warnings in Scripture that no particular individual or even group of individuals are automatically saved. None will automatically enter the future Dominion of God. They must seek first that Dominion and all other things will be added. The various Scriptures referred to or alluded to in the first paragraph of this chapter warn us clearly that there is a prospect of eternal loss. This is one important reason why there was such urgency in the early church to get the Word of salvation in Christ out to the world. A God of love does not desire any should perish, but that all should come to a saving knowledge of God in Christ. Yet without the preaching there can be no such positive response to the gospel. "For how are they to call on one in whom they have not believed? And how are they to believe in one of whom they have never heard? And how are they to hear without someone to proclaim him? And how are they to proclaim him unless they are sent?" (Rom. 10:14-15). Missions is the essential task of the church if the world is to be saved.

Third, we spoke about the future of Israel. Here the discussion in Romans 9–11 was most helpful. It reminded us that God has not gone back on his promises to the first chosen people. Paul clearly envisions a future in Christ for a large number of Jews who are presently outside Christ. This means the church has no business writing Jews off as if they were eternally lost, any more than they should write off any other group of human beings. We also stressed that the New Testament gives no encouragement to racism of the anti-Semitic sort, or for that matter of any sort. The heated discussions between early Jews and early Christians were by and large discussions between two groups of people that were ethnically Jewish. It was an in-house debate about what the true form of biblical religion should look like. This is in fact a very different matter than a modern interfaith dialogue between, say, Jews and Muslims.

Fourth, we stressed that respect for another person's beliefs is essential, even when one must agree to disagree on what is essential to be believed. Interfaith dialogue can be very helpful, as it can establish areas of commonality as well as make clear the differences. In common areas this may lead to groups making common cause on issues of peace, justice, and love in the world. We distinguished between interfaith dialogues and ecumenical dialogues, the latter being between those who are of essentially the same faith.

Last, our discussion of Romans 9–11 stressed that Paul did not affirm the notion of various means of salvation for different peoples, or even several peoples of God, but rather one people of God, whether Jew or Gentile, slave or free, male or female, all united in Christ (Gal. 3:28). This, in Paul's view, is the goal toward which human history is leading and for which we should pray and the shape of the final Dominion of God. There is, however, one more pressing issue that we must address in this study. Is there a future not merely for the world's inhabitants but for the world itself? Are animate and inanimate creation doomed to destruction, or will they, too, participate in the renovation of all things when the Dominion comes?

Questions for Reflection and Discussion

ℭ What do you make of the various warnings in Scripture that salvation is not automatic, and that various persons will in the end not be included in God's Dominion?

ℭ What is the scandal of particularity, and does it need to be overcome?

ℭ Where will the final form of God's Dominion be found, and what is the basis for inclusion in it?

ℭ Is anyone eternally lost because of what he or she does not know about God?

ℭ What is the difference between interfaith and ecumenical dialogue?

ℭ What are the benefits of such discussions?

ℭ Is the New Testament an anti-Semitic book?

ℭ What do you look forward to in the New Jerusalem (read Revelation 21)?

CHAPTER SIX

"On Earth as It Is in Heaven"

W e have been discussing in the previous two chapters the future dimension of God's Dominion. We have stressed both the reality and the importance of that future dimension and how it ought to affect our relationships with non-Christians in the present. But what if we knew that God planned to renew this earth on which we live? Should not that affect how we treat our world as well? I submit that it should, and so it behooves us to explore these issues at this point.

Though it could be said that in the present the Dominion of God exists on earth only in those who acknowledge its saving reign in their lives, yet in the future the Dominion is regularly described in the New Testament as a place that can be entered, obtained, inherited, and the like. The vision of the future includes a time when God's saving reign will spread throughout the earth, when "the kingdoms of this world become the kingdoms of our God and of his Christ."

But if the Dominion of God will be on earth and God will dwell here below, then there will necessarily be some changes in the world in which we live. God in Christ is light, and in him there is no darkness at all. God in Christ is life, and in him there is no disease, decay, or death at all. God in Christ is holy, and in him there is no impurity at all. If God is to dwell with us, not only must we be totally transformed into a truly holy people full of the likeness of Christ, but our surrounding support-

71

ing environment will likewise need to change. God is a God who is pleased when the creation he made is as it was created to be and intended to be. We must explore now the dimension of the Dominion that involves the renewal of the earth in the end times.

The Old Testament prophets often conjured up images of the end time as being like the beginning of time in the garden of Eden. Consider Isaiah 65:17-25:

> For I am about to create new heavens and a new earth; the former things shall not be remembered or come to mind. But be glad and rejoice forever in what I am creating; for I am about to create Jerusalem as a joy, and its people as a delight. I will rejoice in Jerusalem, and delight in my people; no more shall the sound of weeping be heard in it, or the cry of distress. No more shall there be in it an infant that lives but a few days, or an old person who does not live out a lifetime; for one who dies at a hundred years will be considered a youth, and one who falls short of a hundred will be considered accursed. They shall build houses and inhabit them; they shall plant vineyards and eat their fruit. They shall not build and another inhabit; they shall not plant and another eat; for like the days of a tree shall the days of my people be, and my chosen shall long enjoy the work of their hands. They shall not labor in vain, or bear children for calamity; for they shall be offspring blessed by the LORD — and their descendants as well. Before they call I will answer, while they are yet speaking I will hear. The wolf and the lamb shall feed together, the lion shall eat straw like the ox; but the serpent — its food shall be dust! They shall not hurt or destroy on all my holy mountain, says the LORD.

To this we could add the familiar testimony of Isaiah 2:4, which speaks of the time of final judgment, when God will judge between the nations and "they will beat their swords into plowshares and their spears into pruning hooks; nation will not lift up sword against nation, nor will they learn war any more." What is striking about both these passages is that they envision a perfectly good but also perfectly natural new heaven and new earth. Eden, not eternal life, is the benchmark or desideratum here. The first passage speaks of people living out a lengthy blessed life and then dying. Though there is no premature death of young or old, nothing is said about living forever. What is suggested, however, is that the surrounding animal and human world will be at peace, which will facilitate normal lengthy healthy human life. No more human strife is to transpire; no more predatory behavior by animals will transpire. "Shalom" or peace and wholeness in its full sense will have descended on the world.

As beautiful as this picture is, the descriptions in the New Testament go even further, suggesting not merely the elimination of human strife and other causes of premature death, but the elimination of death altogether by means of resurrection. Remember the words of Paul about the resurrection of dead believers in 1 Corinthians 15. In the new earth envisioned by Paul there will be need of neither doctors nor warriors.

Furthermore, the New Testament passages I have in mind suggest the renewal of the earth itself so that the resurrected may live in an environment suitable to their new holy and blessed condition. For example, Romans 8:19-24:

> The creation waits with eager longing for the revealing of the children of God; for the creation was subjected to futility, not of its own will but by the will of the one who subjected it, in hope that the creation itself will be set free from its bondage to decay and will obtain the freedom of the glory of the children of God. We know that the whole creation has been groaning in labor pains until now; and not only the creation, but we ourselves, who have the first fruits of the Spirit, groan inwardly while we wait for adoption, the redemption of our bodies. For in hope we were saved.

The fate of creation and of creatures is bound up together. The effects of the Fall on the world were extensive, and thus we would expect the effects of redemption to be equally extensive. Paul is talking about a promise that creation will one day be set free from its bondage to decay and will obtain the same sort of freedom as God's children will at the resurrection. New persons, made like the risen Christ, will live in a brand new world. And it will not be just a matter of Eden revisited. It will be Eden as it would have become if Adam and Eve had eaten of the tree of eternal life, not of the tree of the experience of both evil and good, including the evils of disease, decay, and death.

So often at funerals we have heard the stirring words of Revelation 21 about the descent of the new Jerusalem and then the voice from the throne saying "See, the home of God is among mortals. He will dwell with them as their God; they will be his peoples, and God himself will be with them; he will wipe every tear from their eyes. Death will be no more; mourning and crying and pain will be no more, for the first things have passed away" (vv. 3-4). If this promise were to come true, it would necessitate not just new persons but a new environment, one free from disease and decay, one free from struggle and strife. Of course, God's permanent residence with his people would also necessitate such changes, for God is holy and purely good.

If we ask why and how this transformation will transpire, the short answer is because of and by means of God's very presence. For example, in Revelation 22:1-5 the water of life flows directly from the presence of God, alluded to by reference to the throne, and this river enlivens and heals all that it touches. It is like the opposite effect to that of a polluted and disease-filled river that defiles all that it touches and all that touch it.

The upshot of all this is that God is the ultimate conservationist or ecologist. This should not surprise us since the God of the Bible is a God who made all of creation and then, when that work was finished, reveled in what he had made, pronouncing it very good. It is also worth reminding ourselves that when the Bible refers to redemption it is creation that is being redeemed, and this entails not just human beings but all of creation. The visions of Revelation 21 and 22 are not just about a new humanity, but about a new creation, a new world.

A moment's reflection will show the wisdom of God's plan. Imagine perfected human beings with eternal life and resurrection bodies who live in a world full of imperfections and disease and decay. Imagine perfected human beings who would have to spend eternity watching all things bright and beautiful and all other creatures great and small continuing to decay and die. This scenario would only lead to eternal frustration and sorrow. It would be only somewhat more preferable than the condition of the Struldbrugs in *Gulliver's Travels*, who have eternal life but not eternal youth and are thereby condemned to getting older and older and more feeble, and yet being unable to die. There is good reason the new creation is depicted in the Bible as one where God will be wiping away the tears from every eye and where there will be no more sorrow or suffering. Eternal life without eternal joy, love, and peace would not be the best of all possible worlds. Eternal life without the companionship of the rest of God's creation would not be life in its fullest form. The Bible does not encourage us to have an egocentric view of salvation, as if it were all or only about saving human souls and letting the material world go to blazes. To the contrary, God has much bigger things in mind for all of creation.

The transcending beauty of this whole vision of the future can also be seen in some of Jesus' brief remarks about the ultimate fellowship meal, the messianic banquet in the Dominion of God when it is fully established on earth. Notice that Jesus speaks of his disciples sitting down with the Old Testament saints such as Abraham or the prophets at table in the Dominion of God (Matt. 8:11-12; Luke 13:28-29). In fact, Jesus himself said that he was very much looking forward to the day after his death when he would once again drink the fruit of the vine anew in the Dominion of God (Mark 14:25). The parable of the wedding feast involving the wise and foolish virgins (Matthew 25) or the parable of the king's wedding feast (Matthew 22; cf. Luke 14:16-24) could also be pointed to, but the images are those of celebration at the consummation of the ultimate union — the marriage of God to the people of God. If there are to be such fellowship gatherings there must also be food, which, unless the menu always involved manna from heaven, requires the good earth to supply such food. All things considered, most of the descriptions of the afterlife strongly favor a less ethereal and more concrete vision of what the final future will be for the world and its inhabitants than we sometimes hear about from our pulpits.

Of course it is right to observe that much of what I have been dealing with here comes in parables or apocalyptic literature. It is more a form of poetry than prose. Thus the temptation is to not take these images very seriously. That would be a significant mistake, for, as we have seen above in regard to Romans 8, we find the very same sort of ideas about the renewal of creation and creature in prose passages. I take it then that we are meant to think that God does indeed have a plan for the future of this material world as well as for his people, even if some of the images used to convey this fact are poetic and not meant to be taken literally. The fact remains that all this material is meant to describe a hoped-for and believed-in future reality that appears when Christ returns and the Dominion of God comes in full on earth. And indeed it will not be exactly as we expect it to be — it will be ever so much more. Eugene Peterson describes the matter as follows:

> Many people want to go to heaven the way they want to go to Florida — they think the weather will be an improvement and the people decent. But the biblical final destination is not merely heaven, it is new heaven and new earth. It is not a nice environment far removed from the stress of the hard city life. It is the invasion of the earthly city by the heavenly one. We enter this final

destination not by escaping what we do not like but by the sanctification of the place in which God has placed us.[1]

What then are the implications of such a worldview, or, better said, Kingdom-view? For one thing it suggests that if we wish to be harbingers for the world of what the afterlife will be like, we would do well to tend and care for the garden God has given us and that we call the earth. It could be said that the doctrine of the resurrection is the ultimate statement of God's concern for the conservation of matter and energy. Nothing wasted, nothing for nought would seem to be his motto. All creation has a purpose, and all of it has a future. Therefore, we must treat that creation with care and respect.

Caring for the earth is not merely sensible for the short term so that our children and grandchildren will have a decent place to live as they grow up. It is also a good witness that we understand that the earth and all that is in it belongs to God (see Psalm 8). We are not owners of this world. We are only stewards and caretakers of it for God's sake. The Bible does not support either a godless communistic philosophy of property and use of the world's resources or a godless capitalistic vision of the same. The Bible suggests that there is neither private nor public property, only God's property, of which we are all stewards. The whole modern theory of ownership is faulty, for we brought nothing with us into this world and will take none of it with us when we go. It also follows from this theology of stewardship that, since the earth belongs to God, we have an obligation to use and dispose of it in a way that glorifies God and helps humankind. The theory of charity too often has as its essential premise "what's mine is mine, but I may choose to share it with you." The problem with this thesis is that the earth is the Lord's and all that is therein. We have simply been entrusted with a

---

1. Eugene Peterson, *Reversed Thunder: The Revelation of John and the Praying Imagination* (San Francisco: Harper, 1988), p. 174.

small portion of it to tend and use for the good of God's Dominion while we are here.

This theological perspective is part of what it means to take seriously the future reign of God on earth, because most assuredly God will hold us accountable for our stewardship of things. This may not prove a very pleasurable experience for those of us who are terribly wasteful. What will we answer when God asks why Americans throw away enough food every day to feed the world's starving and still have leftovers? What will we say when God asks why we support industries that heedlessly pollute our rivers and destroy our air, simply in the name of profit? How will we answer when God asks why we persist in mistreating our bodies by repeatedly eating things that hasten disease, decay, and death in our bodies? If we are supposed to treat our bodies like a temple where God dwells (1 Cor. 6:19), many of us need some reconstructing of our bodies and our chosen lifestyles.

The function of this discussion is not merely theological (to heighten our awareness of what the Bible says about the future of God's Dominion) but also ethical (to heighten our sense of responsibility as those who are to mirror the values of God on a variety of subjects). John Wesley suggested a threefold dictum about good stewardship of the earth and its resources: make all you can by working hard at an honest and honorable trade; save all you can, never squandering money; and give all you can while supporting first your own immediate family, then the household of faith, and then one should do good to all. In his usual memorable fashion Wesley says in his sermon "The Use of Money," which he preached more frequently than all his other sermons except "Justification by Faith," that if you make all you can and save all you can but do not give all you can, you may be a living person but you will be a dead Christian. Lest we arrive at the door of God's Dominion spiritually D.O.A., it would be wise for us to reflect here and now, long and hard on our spending habits and our stewardship of the resources we have in this world. The parable of the talents should not be over-spiritualized. God wants an accounting of what we do with what he has bestowed, involving both spiritual and material resources.

There was once, in my home church in Charlotte, North Carolina, an "every-member stewardship campaign." One of those assigned to go door-to-door at a variety of homes was a young lawyer who was doing rather well in his chosen field, drove a nice car, and wore nice suits. One of the people on his list was a shut-in on a fixed income. When he pulled up to the trailer where this elderly woman lived, he began to feel sheepish about asking her for money and resolved just to visit with the lady and ask if there was anything the church could do for her. After a nice visit, the young man rose to leave, and the lady grabbed his arm and turned him around so that he faced her. She said bluntly to him: "Don't you take away from me my opportunity to give to the work of the Lord. I know I don't have much, but it all belongs to him anyway. Here is my pledge." She understood that God's Dominion over all meant our stewardship of all we have been given.

As part of a work project at Easter during high school I served as a Vista aid in the mountains of North Carolina near Burnsville. It was my task to go back into the mountains and gather up poor children and take them to an Easter party that had been arranged for them. I will never forget one particular family that was dirt-poor. Their house was a shack with holes in the floor, and they lived way back in the hills. Their youngest son, Carl, was about five and had never had any opportunity to play with children other than his own siblings, the family being so isolated. It took a good deal of persuasion to convince his mother to let Carl go with me. Finally she relented, and I told her I would be back very early the next morning to pick him up, as there were many other children to pick up as well.

When I returned early the next morning, Carl had already been sitting on his front porch for a long time. His mother had scrubbed his face red so he would look decent. When I came up to Carl to lift him into the back of the truck, he handed me an enormous goose egg. The one possession Carl had in the whole world was a goose, and he wanted to share its bounty with the other kids who were going to attend the Easter egg hunt. I learned that day that poverty of the flesh can be adjoined to generosity of spirit and that what really matters is what one does with what God has given, not how much one has. Whoever created the bumper sticker that says "Whoever dies with the most toys wins" had surely never caught a glimpse of God's Dominion and his Kingdom priorities.

One of the upshots of the whole line of thinking introduced in this chapter is that we seem too often, especially in the West, to settle for a purely spiritual gospel, a purely spiritual Dominion of God, so that we don't have to deal with the implications of God's Word for our material realities. But if in fact God's reign is a reign over both body and human spirit, a reign over both the invisible and visible realms, over both heaven and earth, then the spiritual-material division of things is unjustified. It is a cop-out meant to help us justify our irresponsibility in the way we handle the material world.

If we examine the gospel closely we see that it is about the salvation of the whole person, both body (at the resurrection) and spirit, heart, mind, and will (beginning here and now). Furthermore, there are even incursions of miraculous healing in the here and now in which God makes plain that he has not given up on embodied existence either. If the Dominion of God is indeed coming to earth in the future and there will be an accounting for what we have done on this planet, it behooves us to recognize the implications of the whole gospel for every aspect of life here and now. The Dominion has a claim on it all.

It is my hope that through this study we have gained a larger vision for the nature, extent, place, and timing of God's saving reign, so that we may adequately pray "Thy Kingdom come" and prepare for that reality in God's own good time. It is also my hope that we will recognize that God's Dominion already exists in our lives and should be celebrated, shared, and acted on. To an extent the Good News is "The future is now." To an extent the Good News is "The future is not yet." As we live in the time between the first and second advents of Christ, we should ponder these things and live accordingly.

Questions for Reflection and Discussion

☞ What does the Bible suggest about the future of the earth?

☞ Will God's final Dominion be of a purely spiritual nature, or will it also have a material dimension?

☞ What does the doctrine of the resurrection of believers suggest to you about God's view of the importance of our material bodies in the order of salvation?

☞ What would the life to come be like if we had resurrection bodies but lived in a still fallen and imperfect world?

☞ If God intends to transform the world into a new creation when Christ returns, what does this suggest about how we should treat that world here and now?

☞ When it was suggested that God is the ultimate conservationist, what was meant?

☞ Reflect on the two stories told near the end of the lesson and discuss what they suggest about our responsibilities of stewardship with what God has entrusted us.

☞ What is the difference between a biblical philosophy of property and material things as opposed to a godless communistic or capitalistic one?

☞ Reflect on what John Wesley suggested in his sermon "The Use of Money." Why is giving so important even for the giver's own spiritual benefit?

Celebrating the Dominion in Kingdomtide

The season of Kingdomtide deserves to be resurrected in the church calendar, and one way to accomplish this would be to preach on the subject during this church season or to use this little book as a tool for an extended series of Sunday school lessons. I would suggest that in the curricular planning seven weeks be set aside during Kingdomtide and that one chapter of this booklet be the subject matter of that week's Sunday school sessions, allowing one week for the Introduction and six for the subsequent chapters.

We also need to develop some rituals suitable for Kingdomtide as we have for other liturgical seasons. I would suggest that it would be perfectly feasible to draw on the existing ceremonies we have in connection with Thanksgiving and incorporate them into the larger period of reflection on the coming of God's Dominion on earth. Thanksgiving is a particularly appropriate time to reflect on the messianic banquet, the goodness of the earth, ecology, and the future new heaven and new earth. The images of harvest and harvest home nicely dovetail with the images of the future messianic reign on the earth and the fellowship it will entail.

Some rituals of renewal would be in order during this season, and perhaps some could be developed for consecration of a new home built through Habitat for Humanity or for the purification of the earth after a church effort at cleaning up a stream or picking up trash in a park or along a roadside. Rituals that help us hallow all of life are worth creating because they help provide a visible symbol of the message of Kingdomtide.

Finally, Kingdomtide is an especially appropriate time for prayer and fasting and the collection of goods and money for others and for CROP walks. The Lord's Prayer and its various petitions are apt subjects for study or proclamation during Kingdomtide. There are many ways we could hallow and make sacred the season of Kingdomtide, reviving and revisiting a forgotten season in the church calendar. It is my hope and prayer we will do so.

Scripture Index